TWAYNE'S WORLD AUTHORS SERIES

A Survey of the World's Literature

Sylvia E. Bowman, Indiana University

GENERAL EDITOR

FRANCE

Maxwell A. Smith, Guerry Professor of French, Emeritus
The University of Chattanooga
Former Visiting Professor in Modern Languages
The Florida State University

EDITOR

Claude Simon

TWAS 346

Claude Simon

Claude Simon

By SALVADOR JIMÉNEZ-FAJARDO

Nathaniel Hawthorne College

TWAYNE PUBLISHERS

A DIVISION OF G. K. HALL & CO., BOSTON

Library of Congress Cataloging in Publication Data

Jiménez-Fajardo, Salvador.
    Claude Simon.

    (Twayne's world authors series ; TWAS 346 : France)
    Bibliography: pp. 199–201
    Includes index.
    1. Simon, Claude—Criticism and interpretation.
PQ2637.I547Z76   843'.9'14   74–30154
ISBN 0–8056–2828–7

To Lisa, my wife

Contents

About the Author

Preface

Chronology

1. *The Wind*   15

2. *The Grass*   35

3. *The Flanders Road*: The Works of Eros   54

4. *The Palace*: Death's Progress   73

5. *Histoire*: The Mosaic of Memory   95

6. *The Battle of Pharsalus*: Confluent Languages   120

7. *Les Corps conducteurs*: Frames of Reference   146

8. *Triptyque*: Multiple Montages   167

   Conclusion   191

   Notes and References   193

   Bibliography   199

   Index   203

About the Author

Salvador Jiménez-Fajardo was born in Spain and has lived in France and Canada before coming to the United States. He took his Baccalauréat at Collège Stanislas in Montreal. He is currently teaching literature and language at Nathaniel Hawthorne College, a liberal arts institution in New Hampshire. He has published articles on contemporary French, Spanish and Latin American novels.

Preface

The ensuing study of Claude Simon's fiction calls for two comments. The first is that it leaves aside all biographical references. As a contemporary writer, Simon's reticence on the possible relationships between his work and other aspects of himself is to be expected. He has made clear statements on the intrinsic limitations of the "life and works" approach, a position with which I concur.

My second comment concerns another element of the more traditional approach to criticism of the novel and is intimately related to the nature of Simon's fiction. The novels that I am to discuss are increasingly self-conscious compositions, in the sense that their true plot resides more in the representation as such than it does in the reality seemingly represented. Indeed, reality appears as a function of form, particularly in the works following *The Flanders Road*. Consequently, in the exegesis of each of these novels, when dealing with its structure, one deals almost exclusively with its plot. The short "abstract" of action presented in the introduction of each study must be considered just that, a fleshless sketch which will hopefully recover its full form in the succeeding pages.

There has been, to my knowledge, no published study devoted entirely to the fiction of Claude Simon. Two books on the New Novel, however, have contained substantial studies of his work. They are *The French New Novel* (London: Oxford University Press, 1969) by John Sturrock, and *Une Parole Exigeante* (Paris: ed. de Minuit, 1964) by Ludovic Janvier. The periodical *Entretiens* devoted Numéro 31 (1972) entirely to Simon.[1] Jean Ricardou, in his illuminating studies on the *Nouveau Roman* has also written at length on him. All of these works, particularly the essays of Ricardou, have had some bearing on my reading of Simon's novels.

The decision to begin with *The Wind* arises from my judgment that the basic concerns of Simon's writing were to appear primarily with this novel (1957, ed. Minuit), at a time when he was struck, he tells us, "by the opposition, even the incompatibility that exists between the discontinuity of the perceived world and the continuity of writing."[2] It was with *The Wind* that Claude Simon reached a greater audience: He was promptly included by critics in the group of the *Nouveau Roman* and has generally remained so classified by readers of contemporary French fiction. Whether such a label adequately defines the endeavors of the writers it customarily includes need not concern us here. The sweep of Simon's vision, in any case, could only submit to the least restrictive of nomenclatures.

My examination of these novels is intended primarily as an introduction for readers whose first perusal might pose some difficulty. Ever concerned with the possibilities of his material—language—Simon leads us from *The Wind* to *Triptyque* along an increasingly single-minded inquiry into its role as the source of invention. Perhaps a straightforward, though necessarily limited, analogy would be helpful here. Simon's fiction moves in a direction parallel to that of some contemporary abstract painting, where canvas allows the artist to examine the virtues of his colors independent of external reference. Language is Simon's instrument, the universe of his novels, a self-referring architecture. In his constant questioning of our most cherished novelistic traditions, Simon requires of us constantly alert attention. Our willingness to pay such heed, however, rewards us with the discovery of the true import of his fiction, situating it in the tradition established by Proust, Joyce, Musil, and Faulkner as one of the great novelistic achievements of the century.

When dealing with works of such compactness, the temptation to analyze at length is difficult to overcome. Yielding to it would have resulted in writing on each novel an exposition that would equal the novel in length. On the other hand, I felt it essential to provide a glimpse of the detailed relationships maintained by Simon's prose. To this end I have generally examined with particular care the opening passages of each work, trying to extrapolate from such examinations some indications applicable to the work's entirety.

This essay is divided into three parts. The first one attempts to establish the themes that have remained central to Simon's fiction as they were first elaborated in *The Wind* and *The Grass*: Eros, death, memory, and representations. The second part examines the three subsequent novels, each from the point of view of one of the motifs previously established, namely, *The Flanders Road*: Eros; *The Palace*: Death; *Histoire*: Memory. The last three novels are considered in the light of the fourth and final theme (representations) according to the scheme: *The Battle of Pharsalus*: Language; *Les Corps conducteurs*: Image; *Triptyque*: Film.

While the pages that follow contain few explicit value judgments, it is hoped that they may offer some intimation of the impeccable coherence of Simon's novelistic compositions, and attest implicitly to the artistic accomplishment that they represent.

I am most grateful to Monsieur Claude Simon for his kindness in communicating to me the biographical information; also for directing me to *Entretiens*, Numéro 31, as well as Ricardou's recent *Le Nouveau Roman*. I wish to thank my colleague, Sam Stark, for his helpful advice. My wife, Lisa Koch Fajardo, typed the initial draft of my manuscript, as well as its final version, with tireless care in her corrections and suggestions. In all ways, her presence was essential.

I also thank George Braziller, Inc., for permission to quote from the novels *The Wind, The Grass, The Flanders Road, The Palace, Histoire* and *The Battle of Pharsalus*. Les Editions de Minuit were also kind enough to allow me to quote from *Les Corps conducteurs* and *Triptyque*.

SALVADOR JIMÉNEZ-FAJARDO

Nathaniel Hawthorne College

Chronology

1913 Born October 10 in Tananarive, Madagascar, of French
     parents.
     Secondary studies in Perpignan, then Paris (Collège
     Stanislas). Studies painting with André Lhote.
     Travels through Europe.
1939 Called into service in a cavalry regiment.
1940 Prisoner in Germany (Stalag IV E in Muhlberg an der
     Elbe). Escapes in fall of same year.
1945 Publication of *Le Tricheur*, first novel, with Editions du
     Sagittaire.
1960 Prix de l'Express for *La Route des Flanders*.
1967 Prix Médicis for *Histoire*.
1973 Doctor of Letters honoris causa from the University of
     East Anglia, Norwich, Norfolk.

CHAPTER 1

The Wind

I *Introduction*

AT the very beginning of *The Wind*, the narrator offers us, in
a parenthetical statement, an explicit commentary on the
text that is to follow. It instructs the reader as to the near
impossibility of organizing the dispersion of memory into a
cogent pattern; the last lines of the parenthesis are particularly
revealing:

(. . . and now, now that it's all over, trying to report, to reconstitute
what happened is a little like trying to stick together the scattered,
incomplete debris of a broken mirror, clumsily struggling to readjust
the pieces, getting only an incoherent, ridiculous, idiotic result; or
perhaps only our mind or rather our pride forces us to risk madness
and run counter to all the evidence just to find at any price a logical
relation of cause and effect in the very world where everything the
reason manages to make out is fugitive and vague, where the uncertain senses are tossed about like floating corks without direction or
perspective, trying only to stay afloat, and suffering, and dying just
to get it over with, and that's all . . .) (10–11).[1]

The quoted passage marks the conclusion of a statement concerning the intrinsic opacity of events, and the difficulties inherent in any effort at an objective appraisal thereof, difficulties
arising from the inadequacy of our senses and our intelligence.
The parenthesis in effect may be considered a "lesson"[2] or "explication" pertaining to the novel in general, and underlining some
ideas to be kept firmly in mind as we proceed. It gravitates
entirely toward the last lines and the idea of a personal, vital
implication on the part of the narrator. He has accepted from
the outset the hazardousness of any logic that attempts to organize
partial visions of a fragmented reality. The narrator himself

15

gives us the two principal instruments of his endeavor: "every-thing—words, images, sensations—vague, full of gaps, blanks that the *imagination* and an *approximative logic* tried to rem-edy" (10)[3]; we soon realize, however, that we deal less with facts than their interpretation, less with events than their plaus-ible or imagined cause and outcome.

Imagination and an approximate logic create the web of poetic intuition which holds together the disparate segments of the novel's development and welds them into an effectively patterned whole. We can already see the effect of the narrator's vision in the development of the "lesson." Indeed, the proposi-tion constitutes an explication not only in terms of what it states, but also through its development. The speaker arrives at his final admission through a sequence of increasingly precise evaluations of his material, until the specificity reaches into him-self and his need to know. Each activity is gradually focused on, with increasing precision: ("what he knew," "what he imag-ined," "to find it, discover it, drive it out,") (10); similarly, the object of investigation is variously specified: ("fragmentary, incomplete knowledge"; "the thousand and one versions, the thousand and one appearances"; "something minute, infinitesi-mal, insignificant") (10).

The conclusion at which the narrator arrives was latent but could only be known as it was verbalized, and he discerns it while trying insistently to capture the exact shading of expres-sion. We have thus the first instance in this novel of words preceding invention, creating the event rather than merely describing it.

As it happens, it is of some consequence that this early passage should reveal to us the manner in which the witness becomes implicated in the action. In effect, were we to consider the novel along the lines of the usual, almost automatic dichot-omy that leads us to visualize the action and its description as distinguishable elements in the composition, his intense involvement would appear less than legitimate. For, as we soon find out, he was not a participant but a mere observer. It is because we are dealing here with writing as a truly "crea-tive" activity that the narrator's implication is comparable to that of his characters. Herein lies also the importance of this passage, for it reflects the very pattern in which the action of the novel is perceived, appropriated, and re-created.

As the novel begins, the narrator listens to the notary[4] in charge of Antoine Montès's estate recount his first meeting with the young man. Having explained to Montès the risks and difficulties of a restoration of his recently inherited vineyard, as well as the advantages of an immediate sale, the notary listens in bewilderment as Montès states his intention to retain it. The narrator's own thoughts alternate with the notary's comments, to establish the background. Montès's mother, still pregnant, left her husband after coming upon him *in flagrante* with a maid; Montès was born shortly after and has never in fact seen his father. His decision to retain the vineyard and administer it, probably at a loss, is all the more surprising.

The ensuing events are similarly presented by the narrator as a composite of his own reflections, the limited viewpoints of individuals whose participation was at best tangential, and his conversations with Montès, whom he has befriended. In the narrator's view, the inability of Montès to compromise coupled with an almost saintlike naïveté upset a delicate equilibrium in the situations he encountered. In his desire to manage his "domaine" Montès dismisses the superintendent and is entangled in endless litigations. He takes a room in a dubious establishment where he becomes emotionally involved with the maid Rose and her two small daughters. She confides to him that her husband, a gypsy, has forced her to conceal stolen jewelry, and he offers to receive it himself previous to returning it to the owner. The police obtain information against the gypsy; as they come for him, he kills Rose, believing she has betrayed him. He is himself shot to death. Rose's two daughters are placed with the Assistance Publique: Montès's efforts to adopt them are unsuccessful, and he finally loses them also. In the meantime, the courts find against him in the matter of the termination of his property's manager.

Other, less overt facets of Montès's influence have in the meantime interacted with these events and are presented by the narrative as their probable cause. Montès is eventually extended an official welcome by the remaining members of his father's family; he is also approached by Maurice, a dubious

individual attracted by the possibilities of gain and intrigue,
who has no difficulty in discovering the details of his attachment to Rose. The narrator sees in these two events the turning point of the drama. The overtures made to Montès by
Cécile, the younger daughter of his distant cousin, afford
Maurice an opportunity to attempt blackmail by stealing a note
addressed to the young man. His efforts are frustrated by
Hélène, the older sister, whom Maurice has already informed
of the questionable associations formed by her cousin. The
narrator does not tell Antoine Montès whether it was Maurice
or Hélène (although he knows it to be the latter) who informed
the police about the gypsy. He prefers to leave this unresolved
in his friend's mind, since the question of guilt does not apply
and Montès, as we shall see, would be the last one to think
of retaliating.

The difficulty of remaining between the extremes of utter
dispersion and implausible compactness is pointed out by the
epigraph of the novel: "The world is incessantly threatened
by two dangers: order and disorder" (Valéry). The two opposing forces find a further echo in the title itself. The wind
constantly blows through the major part of the narrative. It
bends the trees to its will and distorts the appearance of
things; it disperses and erodes with unsettling fury. In the same
manner the drama raced through the lives of its protagonists
leaving but a warped echo in their minds. The "attempt to
restore a baroque retable"[5] is the task undertaken by the narrator, an effort to reconstruct, but also to understand, therefore to control and perhaps to exorcise.

The narrator sees his enterprise as an endeavor to bring order
to a reality that has been exploded by the perennial antagonists
Love and Death, with the inevitable attendance of material
gain. Thus, we have the accustomed elements of a baroque
drama, including the presence of an almost religious figure,
Montès, whose unworldliness approaches a species of laical
sainthood. Also as in baroque drama, the latter's unswerving
rectitude highlights, by contrast, the self-serving motives of
those around him, and he becomes the unwitting determinant
of tragedy. Against these basic forces memory and imagination
pit themselves, trying to amend the distortions they cause in

the perceptions of the characters. The vicissitudes of this struggle form the substance of the narrative.

II *Eros*

The opening words of the novel are uttered by the notary in a conversation with the narrator. His profession, as well, it appears, as his natural bent, lead him to look upon profit as the prime mover of mankind. He sees in the whole drama a simple matter of money, and it is in those terms that he views Rose's designs on Montès; on the other hand, because of her social position, Cécile's own advances are to him simply puzzling. Yet we understand from other sources that it was Montès who first felt some attachment to Rose, in which case the profit motive made no sense, while at least the initial approach by his cousins more probably originated from selfish interests. Still, Cécile herself appears to be wholly free of such motives.

Thus, our first information about the instigations of passion is sketchy and misleading. This matter is for the present ignored by the narrator, his concern with the notary having solely to do with the business of the estate. The possible distortion works both ways: through the professional bias of the notary and through the choice already made by the narrator as to what type of information he will accept from this source. He will himself, however, soon concede the claims of passion as prime mover. The narrator now visualizes Montès descending from the train, struggling against the wind on his way to the notary. As he explores the origins of Montès's appearance in town, his intention is to suggest concurrently the unexpectedness and the inevitability of this event. Montès's arrival is then to become properly a return, and to be necessitated by previous incidents, remote though they may be; it will be unexpected to the town but inevitable to the narrator, that is, to the text. We see quite clearly here the generative activity of the prose, which after having pictured the protagonist arriving, creates for him the need to arrive.

The narrative further elects to emphasize erotic compulsion as its connecting link between past and present, the same element that will join within it other crucial moments. It is general knowledge that Montès's mother parted from his father while still pregnant. As her sole possible retaliation, she left without uttering a word and without telling her husband that she carried his child. This she told later, the narrator says, choosing not to specify how he came to know (although it had to be from Montès), presumably to give his reconstruction a greater appearance of authenticity. Commenting on her outrage, he conjectures that it may have arisen mostly from the irreverence toward the act of love which her husband displayed; she came upon them standing up in a corridor. She must have forgotten, he notes, that man is precisely the only animal who may dispense in his lovemaking with seasons, ritual, and gestures. She did not ask for a divorce, refused any excuses, and would not take any money from her husband or let him see his child.

The narrator then proceeds to establish in the wider context of the town the bond between Montès's coming and the remote incidents preceding his birth. The town is shocked and scandalized by his arrival; by the fact that he should have any claim on his property, especially since his father had allowed it to stagnate precisely because his wife had left him; by his decision to remain; and even more by his looks (clean but thoroughly unassuming), and by his refusal to follow the rules. In contrast to these impressions, the narrator includes a short description of the funeral of Montès's father, where one of the mourners was the deceased's mistress, daughter of his property's superintendent. Although she is young and bedaubed with ill-suited makeup and awkward on too-high heels, her presence causes no appreciable stir. Similarly, in the earlier events involving Montès's mother, people were shocked more by her unyielding attitude than by its cause. The narrator implies that Montès's decision to remain and run his property is felt by the town to be almost a rape or an act at least reminiscent of the circumstances of his own conception: "to undertake, then, the exploitation of a property that was his only by virtue of a nocturnal act (that shadowy obscene brutal and ephemeral thrust and gush, penetration, fecundation of one flesh by another)" (20–21). The idea of an unacceptable outrage perpetrated on the town arises less from the actions of Montès

themselves than from the manner in which they are undertaken, their lack of conformity to convention. It was to the
same feeling that the narrator ascribed the fury of Montès's
mother and her refusal to compromise.

Montès was foisted upon the town as the protracted reprisal
for a sexual indiscretion. His problems with the property's
superintendent are also the result, in part, of a sexual indiscretion; the latter probably felt that certain property rights were
a fair exchange for his daughter. His attachment to the land
has by now acquired a passionate, almost erotic, intensity. The
excesses of passion represent the greatest threat to our conventions, our civilization perhaps, although love itself may
also be its surest binding force. And Montès seems to be the
unacceptable personification of such an excess, an impression
his appearance and his attitude cannot help but reinforce. His
very presence is a threat to public opinion.

Montès's further difficulties also result from a sudden sur-
rendering to passion, although this passion remains unrealized
and is even at its highest moment devotion rather than desire.
He is attracted to Rose's two small daughters as much as he
is to her, and spends most of his free time with them; it is
chiefly for their sake that he offers his help in the matter of
the stolen jewelry. Still, the narrator's implication is that Montès's
decision to remain was also due to Rose's presence: " 'But you
stayed,' I said. 'You already knew you had decided to stay,
didn't you? . . .' 'Yes,' he said at last. 'I think I did know.' And
he began to tell me about the little girl, the older one, Theresa,
. . . and then with no transition he described the woman,
Rose . . ."(79).

In moments of proximity to Rose he feels reduced to the
simplest expression of his being. The first time, this effect is
described in terms whose latent eroticism is easily recognizable:
he feels powerless and hemmed in—"the emptiness, the void,
a kind of dazzling vacuity and he standing, he felt, at its
center, if nothingness has a center, stripped, destitue, fleshless, . . . a rusty nail, a twig, nothing, and beyond the woman,
darkly outlined against the luminous rectangle of the window"
(80). At this point Rose still seems to him an inalterable
feminine presence, as opposed to his own fragility. During their

second encounter Montès sees them both deprived of volition, defenseless against the inevitable onrush of events. The eroticism is now more explicit: Rose confesses her purely sexual, yet absolute submission to the gypsy, trying to shock Montès, whose motives are beyond her understanding. Montès sees that they are all at the mercy of the "drama," like the grotesquely manipulated puppets of the comedia dell'arte. In these encounters Montès appears alienated from events, almost from himself, and yet inevitably trapped in their sequence. His decision to become involved seems to the narrator to be born of unreason: indeed, the clarity with which Montès sees himself and Rose as powerless puppets only underlines the inability of reason to affect in any way the tragedy's predetermined progression.

It is Hélène, Cécile's older sister, who informs the district attorney of the jewel thief's identity. In this case also, outrage is the dominant emotion. She believes Cécile is becoming infatuated with Montès. Maurice has told her of Montès's involvement with Rose and his possession of the stolen jewels. All these facts represent unacceptable threats to Hélène's immutable concepts of form. She had previously caught her maid in bed with a gypsy, whom she later identifies with the thief, and she subsequently sees her younger sister dragged into what she considers to be an underworld of shiftlessness and vice. She herself represents the very epitome of privileged propriety, and looks upon unsanctioned passion as arrant promiscuity. The narrator emphasizes her adherence to social requirements and her implicit belief in class differences. To him these beliefs are but a thin veneer over her single-minded femaleness, through which passion asserts itself: "The spouse, the august and calculating matron rediscovering the harlot's gesture . . . guiding into herself . . . the blind and ancestral bolt" (122.). Even at this basic level, however, the idea of rank and propriety persists (wife—august and calculating matron), as well as that of mythical prerogative, introduced previously through a comparison of Hélène with Juno: "the Juno, the arrogant goddess of fecundity" (119). Hélène's decision is akin to a decree from the gods, the traditional *Dike* become the voice of respectability; a sin against propriety is now analogous to a sin against nature.

The power of Eros manifests itself to the narrator in various manners, all incomplete, from whose juxtaposition and relationships he reaches his own evaluation. In the notary's view, as we saw, Eros is reducible to the profit motive; to Rose it is a physical dependency. Cécile uses sex at the end of the narrative as a weapon against her sister's smugness and the strictures of her social class. In Montès it manifests itself as a profound emotional vortex that absorbs his substance and leaves him empty and weightless, a "twig": it deprives him of his capacity to act, even though its physical demands remain limited. In its wake he sees himself with greater clarity and realizes his powerlessness. For Hélène (and the town) passion must be harnessed by convention. The narrator sees it as the strongest force in the drama, equal perhaps to "public opinion," although ultimately subject to the power of reprisal of public opinion, its most dangerous adversary.

III *Death*

The pervasiveness of death is already felt in the passage which we defined as an *explication* of the novel, where the necessity of finding the logic of events is the alternative to suicidal compliance with their whim. The relation is thus also an effort to see in the central crime a more than capricious outcome. Hence, from the outset the narrative voice assumes the responsibility which in baroque drama was God's, the ultimate ordering agency behind the seeming disorder of life.

Latent and ubiquitous, death will be almost invariably linked to that other driving force whose companion it is, passion. The presence at the funeral of Montès's father of the dead man's mistress is a macabre postscript to the remote circumstances which preceded Montès's birth, and it unites the two forces at the origin of the ensuing drama. This incident is contained within the sequence describing the events, from the past conjugal break to the arrival of Montès, as their natural concomitant.

Consistent with this pattern, the wind-tortured property that is now Montès's, the desolate home where he was conceived, also bears the imprint of death and decay: "[something] dead,

seeming to issue from the apparently uninhabited buildings
with their closed shutters, their bare walls, their deserted
courtyard" (28). The guardian of this bleak abode, the property's superintendent, is variously described as a "cadaver,"
a "skeleton," the human personification of this arid and naked
universe. At dinner with the man's wife and daughter, Montès
recalls that he felt "as though someone had had the fantastic
idea of giving a banquet in the old family vault opened just
for the occasion..." (32). Under the weight of his story and
its foredoomed tragic outcome, the narrator sees death perme-
ating and transforming the very space in which it occurs. The
café where Montès is to stay appears at first deserted and
unwelcoming; Cécile and Hélène's home is reminiscent of a
museum.

The whole town, described as a receptacle of death and of
the tragedies of primitive religion, has become the proper setting for the ongoing drama: "...the city...seemed to drift
within the myriad particles like some ghostly archipelago..."
(44). Drifting in the wind, it recalls the narrator's own considerations[6] at the beginning of the novel when faced with the
crucial task of reconstruction. It is marked by the perennial,
medieval elements of its architecture (dead ramparts, steeples,
churches) fallen into disuse or wrenched from their ties. The
churches appear first "floating keel-upward" (44), performing
an oddly inappropriate balancing act amid the elemental
powers (in this case, passion, death, and greed) they are
meant to withstand and control, as if their purpose had somehow been subverted. Their contents, their substance, so to
speak, seem composed essentially of wealth, ritual, death, and
religious eroticism. The subject of this passion, ritual, and
luxury, Jesus, is an alien presence epitomizing the very opposite
of what propriety and the values of the maintainers of the
churches consider worthy of note. The text very clearly links
Montès with the "sacrificed son" as equally foreign: "naked,
black and Jewish. And he [Montès] sitting in the square or
rather bunched in a corner of the bistro" (44).

The suggestion of impending violence will soon grow
stronger, and become particularly explicit in passages relating
to the sweep of time. Montès anticipates intuitively the inevi-

table conclusion of the drama as an aspect of its passing: "a kind of terror, horror, rebellion ... the cleaving nostalgia of time passing, ... inexorable, definitive" (104). Descriptions of the gypsy and Rose will likewise contain violence and death; "the hum of time mingled with the hum of blood" (92) rushes under the gypsy's skin; green light[7] "plays" over Rose "as if she were a thing, an inanimate object" (102).

However, while the text, and Montès's own sensibility, clearly envision death as a distinctly possible outcome, its actual occurrence strains to their limits the capacity of both. The double death of Rose and the gypsy are first related by the narrator directly as he learned it from Montès. It follows immediately Maurice's visit to Montès's room during which the former ranted at Hélène's trickery (she deftly snatches away Cécile's note). There is no transition to death's presence. Montès relates in the same breath his complete mental exhaustion after Maurice's departure and his sight of the two bodies. An intimate interaction is established between the jumbled facts recalled by Montès and the narrator's effort to restructure them, for it is toward the re-creation, the containment of this particular occurrence that the account has thus far tended.

Yet, the turbulence of the central crime has a disruptive influence on the narrative succession that leads to it. There is a dislocation in the temporal sequence whereby the two chapters following chapter 10 are transposed, the events of chapter 12 properly belong after 10 and those of chapter 11 after chapter 12. The sequence is thus: Chapter 10: Maurice has pilfered Cécile's note from Montès's room; Montès angrily drives him away. Chapter 11: In Montès's room, Maurice berates Hélène for having stolen the note from him upon his attempted blackmail. Chapter 12: The blackmail incident and Hélène's subterfuge are detailed. The beginning of chapter 13 is the continuation of chapter 11: Maurice's rage. The momentousness of the occurrence in chapter 13 requires that the account incorporate its antecedents as they are understood by both Montès and the narrator. In its effort to circumscribe the event as totally as possible, the narrative must now bifurcate to allow for these two sequences. The line of development which follows Montès's own acquaintance with the incidents suggests Maurice's re-

sponsibility. The sequence which is more exclusively the narrator's interposes Hélène's activities and includes her own
responsibility.

The narrative seems first unable to overcome completely the
fragmentation inherent in reality. Death would remain essentially uncontainable, impervious to understanding, rebellious
to the exorcism of words. But the nascent incoherence is harnessed and the dispersion contained with, as a result, a text
that overcomes its obstacles as it creates them, and, while communicating the cataclysmic effect of death, bends death to its
constraints.

Montès's vision of the two corpses under a blood-stained sheet
is the vortex of chapter 13; five times the text moves to it and
recedes, in its search for the most adequate perspective from
which to capture it. It appears first without transition: as
Maurice slams the door behind him, Montès races into the
room where the bodies lie. The second instance maintains the
same suddenness in the main sentence—". . . he seemed to pass
with no transition from the night Maurice had come . . . to
that moment when . . . he burst into the room . . ." (185–186)—
but contains a parenthesis, describing Montès's rush through the
door and the blows he receives from the policeman he has
jostled to enter. The third one includes the thirty-six hours
elapsed between Maurice's departure and his entrance into
Montès's room, as well as Montès's memory of his own mother's
death. The fourth gives the details of the crime itself, the
gypsy's stabbing of Rose and his own shooting by the police.
The fifth and last time, Montès's eyes turn to the corpses from
the morning sun and then to the room whose details he now
notices. Now also, the initial shock somewhat subdued, he
thinks of Rose and finally realizes his intense physical desire
for her: soon after, upon seeing a doll, he remembers the
children. Later, during his interrogation by the police, he
casually mentions that he entrusted the jewelry case to a priest.
The initial shock of discovery and the massive presence of
death are thus gradually mitigated through the addition by
the narrative of an increasing number of attendant thoughts
and details. The very relatedness of these details to the central
fact lessens with each retelling.

The text further presents three approximations to the central event of the chapter, the first two as part of a general interpretation by the narrator of Montès's state of mind during Maurice's visit to his room and immediately afterwards, the third one as a direct quote from Montès to the same effect. They illustrate once more the general organization in concentric movements of description narrowing toward their source, in this case, Montès. We have first an objective, physical description of Montès's body lying on the bed: "The boarding-school cot (almost a mortuary slab: the sheet scarcely disturbed, scarcely raised by the body, drawn smooth up to the armpits)" (181). The clear connotations of death and the very details of the passage announce Montès's later vision of Rose and her husband under a sheet. A few lines later we read a clear metaphorical anticipation of the very circumstances of the crime, this time by way of the sounds Montès continues to hear: "And again only the forgotten tenacious wind outside, ... rustling against the walls like a thief wearing espadrilles ... like time itself passing, irremediably flowing, the blood running out of a wound through which the body empties itself of life in slow despair ... a loose shutter banging or else something falling ... then nothing" (182). The crime could hardly be more vividly announced: "the wind ... thief wearing espadrilles": the gypsy's flight; "blood running out of a wound": Rose's death; "a loose shutter banging ...": the policemen's shots. But here the corpse is Montès, suffering a spiritual agony. This situation is made clear in the third one of these anticipations, Montès's stating that he saw himself "as a kind of corpse" (183).

Yet another metaphorical sequence is developed, parallel to the five reiterations of the death scene, and concerns more particularly the capacity of language to produce such a situation. This progression itself follows five levels of comparison:

(1) P. 184: A comparison between Montès's first vision of the bodies and any account deprived of the elements of syntax (incoherence).

(2) P. 185: Montès's relation of the events to the narrator as a series of disjointed memories, similar to his turbulent entrance into the room (fragmentation).

(3) P. 186: His remembrance of the period preceding the

fated night compared to a story by Balzac where, in a
desire for accuracy, a painter achieves finally an incomprehensible smear (unrelatedness).

(4) P. 189–190: The stately and familiar rhythm of a tragedy, or any ritualized event, opposed to the abruptness
of this particular incident (lack of form).

(5) P. 192: Montès's own realization of the inadequacy of
ordinary feelings (and the words to describe them),
introducing his first examination of the room and a
mental description of its appearance (insufficiency).

Each statement conforms to the particular perspective wherein
the death scene is placed. The fifth one shifts from external
description to personal evaluation, to an awareness by Montès
of his position, and initiates, therefore, a return to the general
development of the narrative. Language has slowly reasserted
its dominance and absorbed the impact of this episode, thereby
safeguarding its delicate and always temporary equilibrium.

In the four remaining chapters death imposes itself in
terms of Montès's continuing mental agony, wherein he looks
upon a cessation of life as the only conclusion to his suffering.
It becomes a boon that is refused him, as is any possibility
of consolation when Rose's children are taken away. He is
destined to remain alone on the ravaged scene; the town, once
more withdrawing to itself, has excluded him, as a cell rejects
a foreign body. Montès remains, like the wind "purposeless,
doomed to exhaust itself endlessly, without hope of an end,
wailing its long nightly complaint as if . . . envying the sleep-
ing men . . . their possibility of forgetfulness, of peace: the
privilege of dying" (254).

IV *Memory*

The narrator acquires his information through Montès over
an extended period of time. There is, then, in the narrative no
true contact with the facts at any moment, no direct perception.[8] We are dealing with language as the stuff of memory,
rather than the transcriber of reality. There is no immediacy
left to the actual events; no residue of reality that has not been
undermined by the uncertainties of time-eroded memory, by

the restructuring power of language. The whole relation appears as an effort to frame appropriately within an inclusive verbal mold the remembered and retold impressions that elusive events have left behind them. It is precisely because of the persistence of imprint of death, and of passion, on the mind that these forces form the two narrative focuses of the novel.

The difficulty of setting Montès and his activity, and its repercussions, into any sort of recognizable pattern impedes the flow of memory and expands the contribution of imagination. His arrival in the town interrupted perennial patterns, both happy and unhappy. In this context, chapter 7, the "lull before the storm," as it were, conveys through the exclusive agency of the narrator the fascination and repulsion which this strange Christlike figure evokes in even the most sympathetic of observers. Neither history nor racial memory, nor individual remembrance, can become inured to him.

This chapter situates Montès's arrival in the larger social context of the region. His difference is not of the type that is historically assimilable by the land, that is, the women, nor does he belong with the new representatives of modernity and greed which seem also to be accepted and even welcomed. After a digression into the characteristics of this new breed of man, belonging neither to history nor to time—the ad men and salesmen born of "the coitus of an automobile and a self-stoking furnace" (109)—the narrator recalls his first meeting with Montès: "... the man in the shop winking at me, indicating with a look of complicity among his pin-ups in bathing suits, Venetian sunsets, and babies on pillows, the figure I saw ... with his long thin body, his wrinkled face, his bony hands ..." (110). Montès stands out against the background of public photographs, an incongruous, oddly aescetic presence. To underline the foreignness of Montès and situate the rejection that he will shortly undergo, the narrator proceeds in this chapter also to the background of Hélène and Cécile's family; this background is in perfect accord with regional tradition: profligacy, greed, social pretensions and a suggestion of scandal are some of its elements. It all belongs to the accepted "memory" of the town; even the latest development in which (a parallel occurrence to that in Montès's own family history), Hélène discovers her maid in bed with a gypsy (Rose's husband), is quickly added with relish to the town's general gossip. It belongs in the category of easily integrated recurring events, as opposed to Montès's return.

Montès and his activity afford the narrator few connecting links with which to forge his causal chain: "reappearing (what was happening to him between times? where was he going? what was he doing? what was he feeling?: what the rumors suggested? what he himself told me? or thought he could tell me? or might prefer to remember? or thought he remembered? or simply did remember?)" (112). The capital importance accorded memory in this admission is undermined by the paucity of available material and further affected by the reticence or selectivity of its main source, Montès. But the narrator does not see his role solely as an organizer of past action; he is principally concerned with discovering that hidden order behind apparent flux, which he seeks in the hidden reality behind circumstance. It is not surprising, therefore, that he makes no mention, for instance, of the possible significance of a phone call that Montès makes upon their first meeting: It could have been important had the narrator really been interested in the events as such, especially since it occurs in his very presence. But he directs his attention to those vestiges of action transmitted by memory and language as impressions and speculations, the very material with which he wants to work.

Since the entire novel is remembered by the narrator, the events as such are situated in a sequence that reflects much more their relative magnitude in his memory than their actual chronology. That is to say, the sequence is more structural than it is temporal. The complete divorce from external continuity that will mark Simon's later works is not yet achieved, however, and there remains some linear development to the drama that language has not completely erased.

The memory that we deal with here is that intrinsic in words and impressions, those of Montès in particular. Of the facts that he chooses to relate to the narrator, he sees as important only those dictated to him by the two overwhelming presences in his memory: love and death. The events that the narrator elects to transmit as well as their sequence are equally under the influence of these two elements, and it is incidents directly related to them that receive greatest emphasis and detail: chapter 13, as we saw, is one such instance where the central vision is five times repeated and evaluated in an effort by language (the narrator's) to remedy the faultiness of memory (Montès's). The most detailed conversations, their particulars not necessarily accurate as to fact but certainly plausible as to connotation, are those in which there is an undercurrent of passion or its frank admission; this concern of the narrator spills over into a scene which is rendered in great detail, mostly imagined, although it does not concern Montès directly: the lovemaking between Cécile and her fiancé.

V *Representations*

It is then to memory that we owe the narrative, but to a memory whose accuracy is dictated by the demands of an "approximate logic," and of imagination; such demands are imposed by the necessity for a cogent pattern, a composition that will go beyond a remembrance to the discovery of its true reality, latent in language. The narrator in his "restoration," his re-creation of events, is well aware of the inner strength of words.

As she watches her father and Maurice from behind closed glass doors, Hélène, unable to hear, sees them talking, "the scene therefore assuming an indefinable quality of strangeness, a disturbing and absurd character, as when the sound track breaks down and suddenly deprives the characters in a film of their voices and they nevertheless continue moving about, their mouths opening and shutting on silence and their faces changing expression, alternately brightening or darkening as if under the effect of drugs or corrosives, as if the lips in parting released with the breath, the invisible air, something stronger than blows, harder than matter itself: words)" (173). Paradoxically, it is precisely through this "silent" scene that the generating power of language is once more asserted. For what we have is a division of words into the constitutive ele-

ments of their effect: the changes that utterances produce in
our facial expression is newly focused upon by our minds,
untrammeled by any sound and meaning; at the same time, it
is as if even through their absence words were capable of
having an impact, as faces continue to move through some
remaining impetus. The running commentary on this soundless
exchange itself communicates sufficient information so that we
have not the interruption of a conversation, but rather both
the conversation and the commentary together. Thus, the text
is the very mirror image of what it describes; the silent scene
proceeds under the momentum of silent words, and the substance
of this description is precisely the effect of silence. The irony is
compounded by the fact that the incident itself involves another
aspect of the impact of words, the note written by Cécile to
Montès which Maurice is trying to use for blackmail. The narrator
has overcome the difficulty of imagining an event on which his
information is both sparse and distorted (he obtains it third and
fourth hand) by accentuating, as it were, the very limitations
of his knowledge. Another effect of this particular "representation" is to isolate the observer (Hélène, in this case)' from
the scene being observed, to install her in a separate time
sequence. Since the narrator must imagine her actions in their
totality (he receives no information from her), his alternative is to offer her as a nonparticipating unemotional presence.
He compares her, in effect, to the blind goddess of Greek
tragedy, imperturbable and marmoreal. Having thus established her as representative of uninvolved and unfeeling Fate,
her later actions will appear both inevitable and arbitrary.

Although an analogy between the incidents of the novel and
the constant flux of a baroque play is established several times,
these comparisons do not fall into the category of what we
would term "representations." They serve rather as a further
expansion of the subtitle of the novel and underline the effort
to create order out of apparent chaos by the baroque connotation of contained mobility. It is, however, in terms of the
total narrative that we can perceive an effort to examine the
regenerative capability of language. The narrator sees his task
as the fusion, through imagination and the power of words,
of the apparently unrelated segments of a fractured "retable."

There develops a continuous tension between the doubly contingent events (fragmentarily known by the narrator, and unpredictable) and the narrative's effort to encompass them through the essentially linear flow of language. Any sort of recurrence or fixity will of consequence be looked upon as particularly useful, and the information transmitted or reiterated will often be disproportionate to the apparent importance of the element under scrutiny. In moments of stress, for example, Montès will focus with great intensity on the details of some scene or image as if he were seeking stability therein. As the narrator points out to the notary: "He loves things that don't move..." (251). When he talks with Rose in what the narrator describes as a strange and nocturnal duo of love (101), Montès notices a lighted shop on the other side of the square: "startling in the darkness, too far away for him to be able to hear, to grasp anything but that mute fraction of life inscribed in the luminous rectangle of the shopwindow" (104). He sees in great detail a number of items in the shop as an arrangement of unusually bright colors; at the back, a curtain opens onto a colorfully outlined scene of domestic furniture and a mother and child playing; still behind, although in the same room, an older woman is seated. The impression is one of endlessly regressing rooms,[9] all sharply hued, brightly delineated. Facing this picture, Montès and Rose sit on a park bench in the night, fearful, full of inexpressible desires, conversing in unfinished sentences, their features hidden by the darkness.

Green is the predominant color in that small oasis of definable forms. It is the color of the countryside in Montès's home. In the constellation of time-related allusions contained in the color green throughout the novel, the one here displayed is that of the vulnerability of the past to time's erosion. The association through metaphor and circumstance of Rose with his mother underlies Montès's relationship with the maid throughout the narrative.[10] His wistful projection of the present plight onto the tranquil mother-and-child scene facing him is apparent— the two women in the scene would satisfy Montès's unconscious wish for a feminine presence combining the role of mother and lover. The temporary imperviousness and comfort of the scene stand also in anticipatory contrast to the desolation of

death in Rose's sparsely furnished room. Soon, as Montès lifts
his head to a "dappled sky" (105)[11] he is captured once more
by the inexorable anguish of time.

The various connotations of greenness represent a particular
use of words and the letters that compose them, whereby
they can be made to project an aura of associated allusions,
here concerning time, and create another level of descriptive
links. In this case the similarity in French of *vert* and *vent*
links the two words together with their correlative *temps.*
Time, like the wind, undermines memory and disperses action.
Green is the color of spring, but soon disappears in this region;
it is impermanent and suggests the vulnerability of nature and
of ourselves to time. By extension, other objects which are
usually green (trees, plant shoots) will also manifest the
connotations of the color itself. The narrator imagines the
gypsy, Jep, marked in death by the epitome of both tokens
of impermanence: "he (the gypsy) barefoot, perhaps . . . one
of those eternal white shirts not even buttoned, opened in a
V on the cinnamon-colored chest" (192).[12] The V is the convergence of both elements in their capitalized initial *vent*
(wind: destruction); *vert* (green: vulnerable time). Near the
end of the novel, Montès is seated alone on a bench: "and
above him the stiff branches, the same leaves he had seen in
bud at the beginning of spring, fragile, downy and pale then,
stiff now, lifeless beneath the shroud of accumulated dust"
(243–244). Wind-accumulated dust has hidden all greenness.

Montès, we know, is particularly inclined to seek segments
of immobility around him, or the solace of repetition. His
only prized possession is a camera whose probable value is
in no way compatible with his apparent lack of means, although
this extravagance accurately reflects the magnitude of his
yearning for fixity. He meets the narrator at a photographer's,
a place where people and objects are "represented," subtracted
from the corrosion of time. The former's own undertaking is
to salvage a portion of the past, partly through photography.
It is appropriate that from their meeting should arise the
narrative, a further effort to fixate time through a representation in words.

CHAPTER 2

The Grass

I *Introduction*

T he Wind clearly represents the first stage in a development that takes Simon toward the totally self-enclosed narratives of recent years, where language acquires *droit de cité* and becomes the novel's major generative force. There is still in *The Wind* an appreciable tension between the momentum of the narrative and the inertness of objects and events; "circumstance" plays a significant role. But already this very confrontation between incidents and the impetus of their description has become an important element of composition; such is particularly the case when the narrative must struggle to contain the explosive forces of death and desire.

With *The Grass,* incident has become more subservient to language and memory. Although the entire novel is orchestrated by the pervasiveness of death, and passion only offers a temporary, insufficient respite, these are now but elements of the heroine's self-evaluation, actively incorporated in her vision. The novel consists of a single narrative bloc, with no chapter divisions; it is given from the double point of view of the protagonist, Louise, and of a narrator so in tune with her sympathies and thinking that the voices are at times indistinguishable. The fiction introduces a set of characters who will reappear, subject to slight variations in kinship, in five of Simon's novels up to and including *Triptyque.* In *The Grass* Louise is linked to this family through her marriage to Georges, Pierre and Sabine's son, who will himself become the central character in later books. Louise's effort to escape the stifling ambience of the home and a pondering of her alternatives constitute the substance of the novel. Upon reflection she realizes that no escape is possible, that her current affair is but a passing adventure, and that she must accept the

35

dying message of renunciation of Great-aunt Marie, the oldest member of the family. All the main sequences in the fiction are linked in some manner with the fact of Marie's dying, or appear overshadowed by it.

The dialogue at the inception of *The Grass* already establishes, as with *The Wind*, the principal elements of what is to follow, uniting under the pall of Marie's dying the four main characters in the fiction: Pierre, Marie's brother, younger in years but toppling toward death; Sabine, his wife, overly concerned with outward proprieties; their son, Georges, inseparable from his mother in Louise's scornful anger.

As for Louise, the kinship she feels with Marie appears not strong enough as yet to deter her from thoughts of leaving. However, the short and ineffective replies by her puzzled lover to her intense soliloquy relegate him from the start to the passive role of helpless onlooker, and although Louise asserts her desire to go, we remain unconvinced. Marie's death is much more present in her mind than is her lover's proximity. Language can occasionally join them, but it more often raises barriers: Louise's voice is now "hard, sad, yet vague."[1]

Louise's thoughts continue to veer towards Marie's death, questioning its meaning for her, delving into Marie's past in an effort to fathom the import of her last days. From Marie, Louise receives an almost valueless ring on the day of her marriage to Georges, and an old cookie box containing the relics of her past, worthless in themselves, entrusted to her by the old woman in her last moment of consciousness. These objects, as well as Marie's agony itself, constantly solicit Louise's reflection and are the origin of all the segments of the narrative relating to the not-immediate past. The other incidents all belong to a period of approximately ten days, starting from the time Marie collapses. The principal ones are: Sabine's loss of her jewels down the drain of a train lavatory and their recovery, except for an emerald ring; Sabine and Pierre's argument concerning chiefly Pierre's supposed infidelities and Sabine's drinking; a fight between Georges and Louise where she tries to taunt her husband into hitting her; and finally the last erotic encounter with her lover, when Louise decides to stay.

As opposed to its explosive suddenness in *The Wind*, death in

The Grass is a transformation, the transition of things that is a constant aspect of nature. We see Marie dying for ten days, refusing to die perhaps, until Louise accepts her burden and the transfer of responsibility for the family's *élan vital* is accomplished, the cycle resumed. And, in effect, the energy that maintains her body in its long agony partakes of the perennial indestructibility of natural forces, of myth: "that continuous, calm and terrible rattle escaping from her lungs like the monstrous respiration of a giant, some playful mythological creature" (18).

Marie's dying is indissolubly linked to time, as the repeated mention of the moving T of light that penetrates her room through the blinds clearly suggests. It belongs therefore to the cycles of history, not that of landmarks and battles, but the vaster, more enduring history of nature, the one described by Pasternak in the novel's epigraph: "No one makes history, no one sees it happen, no one sees the grass grow." It is from this slow but tenacious movement that Louise wants to withdraw; she belongs to it, however, as the text makes clear from the outset: "the grass, the thin tongues of the grass along her bare legs swaying gently—not the breeze but the warm air in its indolent eddies——the high timothy, its supple spidery heads waving, licking her ankles, the multifarious green tongues of the earth, and around her this soft vibration of heat gradually fading, the outlines of things undulating like algae" (18–19). Everything participates in a slow pulsation where the limits between the vegetable, mineral and animal kingdoms are dissolved. The "thin tongues of the grass" acquire "spidery heads" and properties more animal than vegetable ("licking her ankles"): the metaphor is then expanded to include everything, "the outlines of things" (this last word implying also the mineral), while the pervading heat and algae-like movements of "things" suggest the idea of sinking. The world has become a compact, palpitating mass of life, encompassing everything that is subject to the rhythms of time.[2]

The general depiction of the evening scene continues, to encompass in a carefully orchestrated development the arrival of the seven o'clock train. The present participles which concluded the previous passage—swaying, palpitating—(19) also introduce the train's progress. But as it slows down to a stop, the verb tenses describing its movement change to become imperfects, preterites, infinitives, and conclude with a past participle ("the train at a standstill");[3] meanwhile, the human and natural activities surrounding the machine continue as present participles. The syntax accurately mirrors the intrusion of inanimate matter amid life. The train comes nearer nature as long as it moves and becomes an "intruder" when it stops, after a long, almost human complaint: "a long shrill sound, rising higher and shriller, jamming, then nothing, ... at a standstill" (19). When the train departs, the narrative returns to the rhythms of nature.

As the central event of the fiction, Marie's dying remains throughout the vantage point from which all other circumstances are viewed. She was at the origin of the family in the sense that it was through her own and her sister Eugénie's sacrifices that Pierre could become a professor, and consequently win the hand of Sabine, a young girl of the upper classes. Marie remains even now a vital force. She had seen in Louise the only hope for a continuation of this vitality when she gave her the ring. Now, in a more obvious gesture, she presses upon her the accumulated bric-a-brac of her life. Louise understands the meaning of her request and rebels against it: "What right has she? She ... what right!" (99).[4]

The fiction consists of Louise's gradual realization of her inevitable fate as Marie's successor, her weighing of the old woman's past against her own present and that of the rest of the family. Its two poles are hence death, as the end of a process, and transition, the imperceptible passage of things from one state to another, through an apparent cessation, to renewal in a new form. Thus does history grow, like the grass, indiscernibly. Marie's death will therefore not constitute an ending; the dying old woman whom "no one will mourn" (9) at the beginning is at the end mourned by all of nature: "the garden streaming, the whole countryside streaming" (215).[5]

II *Death*

Marie's agony appears some fourteen times in the text, with various degrees of metaphorical development. Its description will undergo subtle transformations, and through them death's forbidding presence will gradually acquire the character of a transitional moment in a ongoing process; the burden it represents becomes then for Louise not only tolerable but inevitable.

The first extended consideration of this event occurs in the early pages; as Louise lingers with her lover in their customary hillside refuge, her mind is drawn to the old woman's bedside. Her relief at no longer hearing the pervasive death rattle is offset by the irresistible attraction that the agony exerts on her imagination. In a series of alternating close-ups and overviews, the text establishes the mutual interpenetration of Marie's dying and the backdrop of living things. At a distance where the sounds of death are no longer heard, sight will become the instrument of ingress to its presence: "From here, at least, nothing more could be heard. Through the trees the car was still visible on the top of the rise, and, to the left, the window with the closed shutters behind which the old woman was dying, motionless . . ." (17–18). The ensuing passage follows a sixfold development with the fourth sequence expanding in its turn to contain a temporal extrapolation: (1) Marie's agony (19); (2) transition to Louise's surroundings and then to the train's arrival; (3) Marie's agony (22–24); (4) the train's departure and surroundings (parenthetically, Sabine's description of the sisters' mausoleum-like home); (5) Marie's room (no mention of Marie); (6) Louise's surroundings (no mention of Louise) (26).

Each one of these segments is submitted in its turn to a process of either magnification or reduction, as the description chooses to focus either on one detail or on a general contour. The train's arrival, for instance, also represents a shifting of perspective to a panoramic view after the detailed rendering of the grass and insects around Louise. The second description of Marie's dying (No. 3 above, pp. 22–24) follows that arrival. It sustains first a gradual expansion from the description of a dried, old hand to the idea of the immutable rites of death, and then a reduction from a statement on movement towards death to the mention of the deformed voices of actors in a tragedy, once more suggesting Marie's labored breathing. The sequence ends with two parallel descriptions of the ambience around Louise and Marie, and no mention of the women themselves. The element focused upon in Marie's room is a T of light pene-

trating through the partially closed blinds, previously characterized as "the initial of the word Time" (18); the one in Louise's
surroundings is a russet cat "still watching, craven and fierce"
(23). The *T* of time suggests Marie's present and greatest
antagonist. The cat, feral, swift, and accusatory becomes for
Louise the personification of her guilt and uncertainty, her enemy.
Its depiction invariably contains metaphors of light (speed) and
explosiveness (death), elements equally contained in the shifting
T of Marie's room. The text itself has thus clearly identified
Marie and Louise from the beginning, echoing Marie's own
previous recognition. It remains for Louise to realize and accept
this identity.

The train, which in this sequence was first present in the
panoramic view following the close-up to Marie's room, also
functions as an element of coalescence, wherein coincide various
antagonistic forces. As we saw, it can participate in death as
cessation, insofar as its stopping breaks up natural rhythms, or
it can be an element of transition, becoming almost one with
nature, when it moves again. Its schedule was interrupted during
the war, when trains became the very embodiment of death,
"still filthy with the entrails of the animals they had been emptied
of (these same animals hanging belly-open and half-butchered
on the posts of the station platforms ...)" (25). Marie arrived
on such a train, unruffled, patient and immaculate after three
days and three nights of chaotic travel. Louise looks upon the
train to Pau as the possible instrument of her escape: "He
promised me we'd move to Pau ..." (15), and Sabine also
echoing Louise's words: "he promises me ... we're going back
to Pau" (56).

As we examine the frequent descriptions of agony, a pattern
appears, reflecting the main features of Louise's encounter with
it. The idea of a titanic, awe-inspiring contest emerges almost
immediately in the first lengthy account of the dying examined
above. Subsequent descriptions continue to focus on the super-
human, mythical aspect of the struggle, characterized particularly by the stertorous death rattle shaking the wasted body of
Marie. The most iterated metaphors refer to ritual and tragedy,
austerity and godlike awesomeness; Marie's breathing is also
repeatedly compared to the bellows of a forge. The contrast

between the fragile body and its fearsome concentration upon death remains throughout; this latter aspect reaches its greatest intensity shortly before the middle of the narrative, in the two sequences where Sabine and Pierre come to see Marie's prostrate form. Under Louise and Sabine's gaze, the old woman's face seems "the austere, arrogant and papery mask of Rameses II . . . stamped . . . with a kind of sealed, almost hostile violence" (85); she seemed to be "rejecting everything that was alien . . . to this struggle" (85–86). Later, as Pierre looks upon his sister, the room appears as "one of those profaned sepulchers . . . : bones, offerings . . . still intact after thousands of years" (87).

From the start, Louise has felt singled out by Marie, who made known her choice of a "successor" when, on her death-bed, she gave the young woman her most valued possessions. The turning point of the narrative occurs on page 104, where, after a detailed transcription of some pages in Marie's account notebooks, we are given in a radical temporal ellipsis a future perspective on the events: "'and later, when Louise remembered that period" (104).[6] In the lines that follow, Louise's memory fuses together visions of dying Marie and of herself running away from the house, down the hill toward her rendezvous, her heart beating to the rhythm of Marie's breath. This flight, the moment when her identification with Marie appears for the first time to be almost complete, also represents her most intense moment of rebellion: "'She's nothing to me, she can't, she hasn't any right'" (105). But the cat is once more there, "the sharp, yellow, fixed stare seeming to clutch at her" (105), and the grass "licking her bare legs" (106), all of nature belying her refusal, changing, imperceptibly shifting from transition to transition.

Seen from the future, the rebellious element in her confrontation with Marie's approaching death, although not minimized, seems now futile. The emphasis will shift in descriptions of it, with greater stress falling on the frailty and vulnerability of the wasted body. What we realize now, in this second half of the novel, is that Louise looks upon the decision to stay as entirely her own. The awe she felt before Marie's struggling body is mingled again with pity, as it was in the novel's first lines. The old woman's agony affects everything around her, but as it does so, it loses some of its forbidding aspects: "... the old, fragile heap of bones, skin, exhausted organs yearning for rest, for the original nothingness, lying—barely raising the sheet—at the heart, at the center of the house, reigning, invisible and omnipresent, not only over all the rooms (presiding—without needing any grace said—at meals, at the common breaking of bread in the familiar clatter of plates, together, during the other old woman's ridiculous chatter) ..." (119).

Three important ideas appear in these lines. There is, first, the new emphasis on the brittleness of the body and on its wish for death. Also, the connotations of divine presence, although they remain, have undergone a slight change, Marie becoming now a possibly intercessionary divinity (communion is suggested here), a more accessible being. Finally, even though it is by means of a contrast, her presence is said to preside over the "other old woman's ridiculous chatter"; it is contiguous to that of Sabine, tinged within it some way. (Also, the words *old woman* are used for both.) The possibility of Marie's death becoming a transition is now greater. In fact, Louise is remembering all this now (the idea of a future remembrance is reiterated frequently from page 105 on) from a vantage point where she has already accepted her fate. It is this acceptance which has begun to erode Marie's domination, slowly depriving her death of its mythical connotations to transform it into the passing on of an old woman. Indeed, Marie is situated here squarely within the generally deteriorating ambience of the family; it is the only time when Louise speaks of them together at the dinner table. She also includes a description of Pierre, "the man-mountain" (119), imprisoned by his obesity, and of Georges, whose delicate thin "pianist's hands" (120) are blackened by the sun and machine grease.

The impinging of the family's vital decay upon Marie's previously majestic end allows it to return to human proportions and to make Louise's assumption of Marie's burden not only possible but necessary. Louise's next visit to the dying woman occurs immediately following an altercation with Georges, where she admits her plans to leave with her lover. In this scene, as Georges displays his antagonism toward his father and his hatred of all things intellectual, his abnormal muscular development, the result of his fruitless labors in his blighted orchard, appears ill-suited to his slight frame. This visit is also preceded by Louise's accidental eavesdropping on an argument between Sabine and Pierre; in the incident Sabine displays her worst characteristics (overindulgence in drink, selfishness, vanity, unaccountable jealousy), while Pierre appears almost immobilized by his corpulence. When Louise now looks upon Marie in the lamplight, "as if death had something indecent about it" (137), the old woman seems to have become "even more dessicated, shrivelled, wizened, so that it seemed more than ever out of proportion with the deathrattle" (137). The scene has acquired some of the unseemliness of the previous pages, the body shrunk to its natural fragility. The *T* of light which at the beginning epitomized her stubborn struggle against time has been replaced by the discreet hue of a shaded bulb. Louise now feels exasperation rather than awe upon hearing such an unlikely rasping sound emitted by so brittle a frame, a sound that is now for her an unfair beckoning; she leaves in a "wave of rebellion, of rage, of despair" (138). The gradations of emotion, from revolt to despair, are three of the four main sentiments that have grown within her through her confrontation with Marie; a last one, resignation, is shortly to impose itself.

It is at the height of Pierre and Sabine's altercation, when Louise can imagine them "tragic and yet grotesque" (188), that a parallel description of Marie suggests the moment when the transition may be accomplished. At this point the struggle between Pierre and Sabine is rendered in terms of an old painting in a museum, the visitor "trying to remember what ancient king and queen . . . struggled, were condemned to struggle eternally" (187), amid the silence. In the vision of Marie's agony that follows, the skeletal, prostrate form is related to her same youthful self examined by Louise in an old photograph, as well as to the picture of a demure young maiden on the box of trinkets now in her hands. This picture is an endlessly receding perspective, the girl holding a box with a girl holding a box, and so on. The text establishes here a transition through various ages (death, old age, middle age, youth) and various representations (painting, description of the agony, photograph, picture on the box). All is contained within the vaster representation that the fiction itself is, whereby the crucial transition (death to youth) between the dying Marie and Louise is also achieved. To pursue and affirm this transition, in a struggle during which her mind is filled with the turbulence of Pierre and Sabine's own fight, Louise feverishly demands of her lover that he possess her, knowing now that she will not leave with him. The transfer of roles, of substance, almost, has taken place, and Louise has reached within her the plane of resignation.

In the last description of Marie's death, all stateliness has vanished. Once more, it occurs amid further manifestations of the family's deficiencies. Georges's presence is perfunctorily suggested when the pump which he has stubbornly been repairing stops once more. Pierre is seen laboriously rising from his seat, searching for his pen amid scattered sheets of writing. But it is the old woman's convergence with Sabine that is underlined, both now equally expendable, equally spent in Louise's mind. To emphasize the barrenness of their condition there precede a few lines about a pregnant maid at her chores. In contrast, Marie is dying a childless old spinster; Sabine, painted and bedecked like an ancient priestess, appears now subjected to her own protracted agony. After this transitional moment when youth becomes death and life turns into a representation (painting, photograph, etc.), Marie's presence continues to diminish, as Louise's revolt is changed to despair and then to resignation. In the concluding lines of the narrative, the train arrives on schedule, and with it the suggestion of inevitable repetition.

III *Eros*

The centripetal pull of Marie's agony subjects to itself and distorts every emotion in the narrative. As a consequence, the latency of death at the very heart of erotic involvement, a motif already basic to the structure of *The Wind*, becomes paramount in *The Grass*. As for cessation and transition, the two aspects of death pertinent to this novel, it is paradoxically the first and totally negative one that eroticism here contains. Passion appears a drive both repressed and spent, manifesting itself in emotional aberrance and patent sterility. In this sense it stands in opposition to the concept of the old woman's death as a transfer of roles. In effect, it is between these two antagonistic forces that Louise will be torn, dismayed and repelled on the one hand by the futility of her existence as Georges's wife, restrained from flight on the other by the presence of Marie.

The lines of the contest, which appear clearly drawn from the beginning of the novel, are only temporary. As the narration progresses and Marie becomes more vulnerable, more accessible, partaking of the failings of the household, Louise will be able to overcome her awe and see herself as the old woman's successor. Although it was Marie's dissimilarity with her kin that first won the young woman's affection, it is her ultimate susceptibility to their human frailty that in the end earns her Louise's allegiance.

Hence, at first it seems to be between her respect and affection for the dying Marie and the impulse to follow her lover away from the pall of her married life that Louise must choose. But already the latter alternative is shown to be at best makeshift. In her early encounter with the young man, she uses him as an excuse to verbalize her thinking about the situation, twice within a few lines looking beyond him at "something in front of her which he could not see" (10); later on the text erects a wall between them: "... and between them the sky was once again like a plate of glass streaked every which way by the dark lines of the branches" (14). These black lines, suggestive of the function of words themselves, will continue to separate them to the end. Louise does not want to go with him because she loves him, rather because she abhors her present situation.

The background against which Louise's concerns take shape manifests the results of Eros denied or distorted. Marie's life has been one of constant renunciation, all possibilities of love subordinated to the demands of her brother's education. Sabine's love for her husband Pierre is exhausting itself in outlandish outbursts of jealousy. Georges's love for Louise appears now to have been secondary from the beginning to his need to rebel from the family's traditions. Louise belongs to another class, just as Sabine once belonged to another class; but whereas Pierre's promise allowed him to raise himself to a "higher" milieu, Georges, in his condemnation of all that his father

stands for, selects a less privileged wife. The futile exertions
of these repressed or misdirected passions are in the narration
an expression of the negative view of death held by the principal
characters, including Louise herself until the closing moments
when she accepts being Marie's successor. It is her desire to
escape from the stifling sterility of her marriage and her
husband's home, her yearning to live unconfined, that throws
her into the arms of a lover. Alone in the house when Marie
suffers her seizure, avid for any possibility of freedom, she sees
in the dying form a portent of her own end; awe and repulsion
enhance in her mind the impenetrable, almost mythical aspects
of that ultimate struggle.

Sabine, in her drunken incoherence, interrupts her diatribe
against Pierre with a tortured wail, the only words born of
her true anguish "I don't want to die" (145). Her bright
dresses, her exaggerated makeup, her drinking, all are efforts
to resist time, hold the end at bay; but they can only make it
seem more imminent; the ornaments of eroticism are now an
aimless masquerade.

The house, the countryside itself, have become inadequate
environments for the natural cycles of fructification. Georges's
incapacity to obtain full maturation from his pear trees is a
reflection of his personal failure with Louise, she being both
childless and dissatisfied. This climate of domestic decay is
forcibly set forth during the doctor's visit to Marie's bedside
immediately following her collapse. In the night air, the penetrating odor of rotting fruit overpowers the accustomed aroma
in Marie's room, "that fragrance, like the smell of a dried rose"
(10), a scent of still life that the old woman seems to have
brought with her from her ancient rambling house. The doctor
comments on Georges's misuse of the land and informs Louise
of his increasing gambling debts; other comments on the
family's fortunes lead him to test the young woman's feelings:
"'I wonder what got into you, what you thought you were
doing, marrying into a family like this. . . . You know how
lovely you are, I . . .'" (73). Louise remains curt as she shows
him the door. The kinship between thwarted love (here the
result of Georges's insufficient concern), and the more negative
component of death, true cessation or interruption, is evident

throughout this scene. The doctor has declared Marie effectively dead, although she continues to breathe. Louise cannot accept this; she sees Marie's eyes open, hears her powerful gasps, feels her presence still. The man's advances repel her; beyond their irreverence they also represent a translation into erotic terms of his assumption of Marie's death. Louise's refusal is aimed at both these connotations.

From the outset it is her affection for Marie that Louise views as her only bond to the family: the ring she receives from her becomes a more potent symbol of allegiance than the one affirming her marriage. Both in effect bypass Georges's role: Louise's wedding ring was chosen by Sabine and bought with her money. It is actually between the antagonistic power of the two old women that Louise is at first divided, repelled by Sabine and attracted by Marie. The men are of little importance, and Georges himself hardly counts in the narrative. The opposing characteristics of Sabine and Marie on the other hand are clearly delineated: Sabine is religious, excessive, and weak; Marie is resolute, measured, unassuming, and a convinced unbeliever. Louise will waver until she can reconcile within herself and supersede these two conditions.

As we previously saw, Louise's first words in the novel, addressed to her lover, refer to Marie's lonely death. From that moment Marie's ascendancy in her mind will increase apace, aided by Sabine's own temporary absence from the household. When Sabine returns, her influence makes quick inroads into Louise's concern for Marie. One of Louise's last meetings with her lover begins with her comments on Pierre and Sabine's argument of a recent evening. After she discovers in the account notebook Marie's old photograph, which combines in the dying body the vulnerable hopes of youth with death's austerity, Louise understands how Sabine herself and Marie partake essentially of the same nature, bear the same burden. In the final, feverish encounter with her lover, their futile embrace encompasses for her the lifelong frustrations of the other two women. As she makes love, she thinks of Sabine and Pierre's struggle; later she tells herself "Now, now I'm dead" (205), her prostrate body a replica of Marie's. The synthesis has been accomplished, and through it, the protracted transition. The old woman may now die.

Love reduced to its most limited aspect, where all that remains of it are duties without joy, becomes a yoke, our bodies the mere instruments of obscure natural ends. Copulation comes to be the correlative of death's negative face. As an instance, while Pierre examines Georges at the dinner table, Louise ponders what possible rapport there can be between the two men, what possible link, remaining from that "spasm (like, comparable to, a brief death, a sudden annihilation:)" (121), at the moment of conception. At the opposite pole is Marie's agony, one which ends only when her true successor accepts her role. The result of this sexual encounter was Georges, as the new Louise will be, in some sense, the outcome of Marie's protracted death. Thus, paradoxically, intercourse becomes an interruption, and death a continuation.

Uniting within herself both opposites of this paradox, as she does the antagonistic natures of Marie and Sabine, Louise is able to become the indispensable element of continuity in this minute fragment of history. Lying on the grass after making love she is now closest to its cycle: "lying there motionless, spread out, and at the center of her body gleaming palely in the twilight, that spot, that black triangle, dark and wild and shaggy" (205).[7] Louise's submission to deathlike transitory passion has been incorporated by the text to the continuity of living things, her *mons veneris* assuming the characteristics of surrounding vegetation, the grass of history.

IV *Memory and Time*

Louise's initial rebellion is reflected in the narrative by her emotional reaction to the impervious movement of natural things. Early in the novel, as she stands in the thicket with her lover, the endless, indifferent flight of insects moves her to near despair: "... the insects ... circling ..., one of them projected into the light, making a gray-mauve S ... the insects still circling ... as if they were compelled to fly without a purpose ... continuing heedless in the descending sun, heedless ..." (20).[8]

The narration shifts without transition from that aimless dance to Marie's hand, "moving back and forth over the sheet" (20). The S drawn by the insects against the light is the last letter of the word *temps* ("time") whose initial *T* crawls daily across Marie's room. Inexorable time also links the two women, although the dying one may appear at first to have mastered it, "assuming day after day that majestic and timeless aspect" (21), and the young one seems to dread it.

With respect to memory and time, the first stage of the central transition in the narrative occurs through the automobile trip from the house to the train station, from the presence of the dying woman to that of prostrate Sabine. The speed and silence of the journey, as well as the similar situations at either end, give Louise the impression of having simply moved from one room of the house to another: "Two closed rooms, then, two silences" (77). In both situations there is a conjunction of time-related elements: Two eighteenth-century clocks, pointing out, not the passage of time, but its repeated circuits, "the essential thing being the fact of the face and the hands, that is, the notion of a closed circuit" (77). The incessant clanging of trains in the station tells a time "no longer ... doled out ... but marked by the slow displacement of monumental and luminous hands suspended, in the night on the pediment or the belfry of the station ..." (77), and where, to remind us of the wartime train that brought Marie to the house, it is also "lugubriously punctuated by the distant and sporadic lowing of cattle forgotten on a siding" (78). At this moment, the narrative shifts for a few lines to a unique present tense, when the clocks are "both there to impress insistently on the mind of the traveler or of the clandestine lovers that furious and panting anguish of the provisional" (78)[9].

This trip, returning the older couple to the family home, introduces therein the presence of Sabine. The life of the two old women appears now epitomized by their most precious possessions. Marie's account books, with endless rows of dates, expenses, and tasks, objective and cold, are a distillation of time, the precedents of her agony; Sabine's jewels (whose loss caused her own temporary prostration) represent the result of eons of mineral purification. The stones are returned to her in a small sack, a slight dusting of flour on the precious contents attenuating their brilliance; this detail prefigures the forthcoming fusion in Louise's mind of what the two old women represent: toil and luxury.

Previous to the return of Pierre and Sabine to the house, the fiction was heavily weighted towards the past. Immediate events were rendered in the preterit, with long descriptive sequences in the present participle, many devoted to Marie's past life. Now the movement to the future becomes evident, the temporal point of view shifting seemingly to a moment late enough in time to afford a more detached vision.

It remains for events to shift from the realm of remembered fact to that of the unexpressed, denoting exclusively the movement of Louise's thought; "not an incident . . . occurring on a specific day, but something latent, something permanent, established" (126). This progression will thus mark the changes in Louise, from reluctance to revolt, acceptance, and finally resignation. Likewise, as the narrative reaches ahead, it establishes the fiction clearly as a construct of Louise's memory, of her thought, while incorporating its development into that of the family's history, and the latter into the inexorable rhythm of growth and decay.

V Representations

Accompanying the first definite modification of temporal point of view, the narrative undertakes a striking spatial translation, whereby an extended panoramic view joins distance in space to distance in time. The sequence is introduced by some comments on the powers of our mind, "that terrible machine for assimilating every new situation" (88), easily understood here also as the narrative voice. It is contained within two metaphors that underline the idea of slowness: the first one refers to all-encompassing consciousness, whose characteristics are "this sort of torpor, of sluggishness, this boa's somnolence" (89); the concluding image notes the movement of the T in Marie's room: "creeping across the room, patient, reptilian" (92–93).

All the elements of the narrative within these two points are subjected to radical alienation; time is seen as a sequence of long drawn-out days that affects all spatial coordinates: "the slow days following each other, passing, swallowing up branches, hills, . . . life . . . manifesting itself only by rare, sporadic, insignificant and brief appearances, . . . so tiny that they seem to emphasize still further that huge disparity between our actions and the immensity at the heart of which they are immersed . . ." (89). The distance of narration is also changed, the narrative voice assuming a new objectivity, choosing to infer, for instance, that this house (so intimately known at other times) is inhabited only because of its visible open shutters. From afar, the identity of its people is no longer certain, their activities unfathomable. Then, imperceptibly, the text moves closer to its subject. The inhabitants of the house are involved in recognizable actions, and we enter the house itself to Marie's room, by the intermediary of the closed shutters[10] through which the sun penetrates in the form of a *T*. Ironically, the text, which has surmised "life" in the house from open shutters, chooses to enter it through the closed ones of the death room. Through this alienation the representation unveils its inner functioning, pointing out the gains and the losses inherent in the choice of point of view. Here, although the distance has allowed perspective to enter the picture, signaling "that huge disparity," it has also allowed most of the substance to escape, the text in effect losing its voice, like a play out of earshot whose actors "far from resolving the mystery, darken it still further" (80).

After this passage, illustrating the alternatives of the spatio-temporal point of view, the text explores other representational elements, where the idea of temporal distance is allowed to affect the material organization of the book itself, that is to say, the ordinarily inevitable linear disposition of prose. As Louise examines the contents of the old box given her by Marie, the enumeration of objects and the rendering of the contents of the notebooks impose their own unfolding on the paginal layout. As in the previous instance of narrative relativism, the effect becomes more noticeable as the text proceeds. We find first a list of the objects contained in the box, with one to five lines devoted to the description of each. The

spacing is already in marked contrast with the massive appearance of the preceding pages. There follow, interspersed among
the usual long paragraphs, lists of dates (years) in blocks
of several lines, and later fragments of monthly accounts and
their sparse comments. The last entries afford the greatest
amount of blank space on the page, and are followed by the
running text at the moment when the narrative projects Louise's
thoughts decisively into the future (104).

The contrast between the two aspects of the text is not
merely one of arrangement and apparent content. It also arises
out of the clash between the visions of duration they represent.
On the one hand, in Marie's possessions, there is an extreme
compression of time, filtering out the very substance of life
to the point where the death of her sister Eugénie becomes one
line-long entry among others. On the other hand, in Louise's
thoughts, the days of Marie's agony, seen from the future,
appear "not like a specific slice of time, measurable and limited,
but as a vague, criss-crossed interval, composed of a succession, an alternation of ups and downs, of darks and lights"
(104–105). This very metaphor underlines the striking difference of import of the "darks and lights" as it suggests that we
take into consideration the text in its totality, both as visual
arrangement and content. These two instances of contrasted
time-perspectives occur at a point where, as we pointed out,
the narration is progressing towards the focus of hindsight,
and the setting of its elements definitely within the breadth
of memory. They offer alternative spatiotemporal dispositions,
concentrating their effect upon this crucial moment of transition in Louise's attitude, and establishing in the foreground
once more the primordial importance of the narrative as such.
Louise's search for a way out is thus reflected by, and almost
subservient to, the formal experimentation of the text.

A similar graduated penetration of the contents of the box
and the text of the notebooks precedes the discovery by Louise
of the old photograph where Marie appears in full youth.
Words alone, although they crystallize memory and imagination, are not sufficient to dissipate Louise's resistance. They
need a more palpable ally, other material with which to increase their effectiveness. It will be provided by this photo-

graph. Another photograph had previously been the object of her close examination, one taken on the occasion of Pierre and Sabine's marriage, but Marie's appearance in it held no mystery, her face "already looking a little as it was going to be later" (63). The one she finds in the old woman's notebooks, however, gives the latter a thoroughly unexpected dimension. Still quite young, she seems to Louise to be looking at a young man with some interest. The discovery of this unrealized possibility in Marie's past, as well as her strikingly youthful appearance, give back to her life the content of which it had been deprived by the endless columns of accounts. It is after this that her agony is denied all its forbidding mythical connotations, while she becomes more vulnerable than ever to the undermining influence of Sabine's failings. Thus, by opening a wider door into her past, this last factor assures Marie's longed-for future, as it provides the final component of Louise's assent.

CHAPTER 3

The Flanders Road: *The Works of Eros*

I *Introduction*

IT is in *The Flanders Road* that reality becomes entirely
subservient to the creative activity of language. The influence
that events had on the narrative flow in *The Wind* and *The
Grass*—and we saw that, especially in the latter novel, it was
already minimal—has now vanished. In this third novel words
have achieved complete autonomy; they conform exclusively
to the reality that they themselves give birth to. Simon is clear
on this point: "Each word brings forth (or commands) several
others, not only through the strength of the images that it
attracts to itself as a magnet, but sometimes also through its
mere morphology, simple assonances that, as with the formal
necessities of syntax, of rhythm and of composition, often
reveal themselves to be as fecund as its multiple meanings.
Thus were written *The Flanders Road, The Palace,* and *Histoire*
even more."[1] In *The Flanders Road* language is a corollary of
remembrance and creates its own actuality out of disconnected
memories; but the story is not merely a recall of the past;
rather it takes shape as it is read, reflecting no presence but
its own.

What we have is a series of moments in a memory, linked
together by associations that are often fragile, and whose
chronological sequence can be but an approximation. The
temporal structure is here completely self-contained; that is
to say, it reflects not an external order of events but the
internal movements of the narrative. The fiction develops
mostly as the protagonist's reflection upon a number of incidents, a purely personal interpretation. This central character
is Georges, whom we saw as Louise's husband in *The Grass.*
Other elements of the previous novel reappear in *The Flanders*

54

Road: Sabine and Pierre are recognizable as Georges's parents, and particular mention is made, for instance, of the former's shrillness, the latter's obesity and intellectual entrenchment. But whereas earlier pervasive death was the underpinning of the novel, it is here passion that exerts the greater influence, although large segments of the action deal with war.

The aim of Georges's reflection throughout the narrative is to ascertain whether de Reixach, his captain, allowed himself to be killed. Except for a few pages at the end of the novel, this reflection takes place while he is in bed with Corinne, de Reixach's widow. The possibility of de Reixach's death being a suicide because of his wife's infidelity, and the fact that this event remained foremost in Georges's thought while death assailed him on all sides, establishes passion as a crucial element in the novel's structure. This is further emphasized by the very circumstances of Georges's recollection, with Corinne's arms as the point of departure: "... what had I looked for in her hoped for pursued upon her body in her body words sounds..."[2] (279–280). Three narrative sequences remain in the foreground of the novel, ceaselessly reviewed by Georges's memory:

(1) Disconnected fragments of his wanderings during the 1940 retreat in Flanders, accompanied by Captain de Reixach and three comrades from his squadron (Wack, Blum, and Iglésia).

(2) A period of imprisonment in a concentration camp in the company of Blum and Iglésia.

(3) Events of a supposed historical nature, soon expanded by his imagination, dominated by the figure of an ancestor of the French "Convention" period.

Other less important moments recount incidents of Georges's home life previous to the war, his flight after the initial rout in Flanders, and with Iglésia after de Reixach's death; also the race in which de Reixach insists on riding a nervous chestnut filly, and George's journey to a concentration camp in a cattle train. From the second half of the novel, his returns to the present and his sexual embraces with Corinne increase in importance until a few pages before the end when she leaves him. All these scenes are re-created with elements that

range from probable fact to sheer imagination and are constantly reinterpreted, so that there never seems to remain any
constant residue of experience.

The novel is divided into three parts of unequal length, each
one preceded by an epigraph relating to either love or death.
This association of love with death is manifest throughout
the fiction, Georges's mind preferring to linger on incidents
that contain or suggest both. The epigraphs themselves clearly
stress these ideas. The first one is from Leonardo da Vinci:
"I thought I was learning how to live, I was learning how to
die." The second, a longer statement by Luther, presents an
ironic view of sex; the last one, by Malcolm de Chazal, contains
the thoughts of the previous two: "Sensual pleasure, volupté,
is the embrace of a dead body by two living beings. The
'corpse' in this case is time murdered for a time and made
consubstantial to the sense of touch."

The novel begins as de Reixach shows Georges a letter from
Sabine in which she points out their kinship and, we surmise,
suggests a more than official bond between the captain and
the recruit. Georges's whole reconstruction, his effort to interpret de Reixach's absurd death is also aimed at ridding himself
of the curse that indirectly affects him. The implicit accusation
that he directs at his mother from the start—he is furious at
the letter—is born of an instinctive pride which he wants to
smother, of belonging to this aristocratic family. That is why
he wants both to despise them and to justify their actions.

The narrative will in part arise from the struggle between
these two tendencies in Georges, both epitomized by Corinne:
on the one hand, "the most Woman of all the women he had
ever seen" (140) for Iglésia, and Georges's sexual ideal during
five years; on the other, perhaps nothing but a capricious,
amoral woman. The very occasion of Georges's reconstruction
imbues the text with sexual connotations which lift this contest
beyond the confines of Georges's and Corinne's personalities.
We shall examine some aspects of the dualities, Eros-death
and Eros-tradition, as well as the relationship between Eros
and memory, emphasizing in each case the fundamental role
of generative language.

II   *Eros and Death*

The conception of love that prevailed in *The Wind* and *The Grass* allowed for some positive elements, which, though they remained latent and did not affect the generally calamitous outcome, palliated somewhat the overall pessimism. Montès's devotion was genuine if misguided; Louise is drawn to Marie and admires her, until she thinks the old woman's demands are unfair. Insofar as affection remains free of the immediate impositions of erotic ardor, it retains a positive potential. In *The Flanders Road,* where passion only remains of love, it is more than ever an ally of death. Only as the enemy of tradition and rigid form does it bear affirmative results.

Three principal episodes establish in the novel the link between love and death, with the latter either a concomitant or a consequence of the former. The first one is an incident during the retreat itself, when a young country girl brings some light to the barn where the four soldiers are to spend the night. The dominant characteristic of Georges's memory is visual imagination. His remembrance of the young woman takes a comparison with a painting as its point of departure, the scene similar to "something like one of those old paintings executed in gravy" (38). The warmth of the barn is then described in almost sexual terms, focusing on the girl's body, "all her flesh swollen by that tender languor of sleep" (38). After a second comparison of her illuminated form with the light of a canvas, she disappears into the dawn "like a cataract on a blind eye" (39). Georges continues to see her in his mind as he proceeds to prepare for rest. She has remained "not a woman but the very idea, the symbol of all women" (41), and he now molds her in his imagination into an elemental, primitive statue. Its center is "that thing with an animal's name, a term of natural history—mussel sponge valve vulva—" (41), from which is born the innumerable breed of armed men that swarm over the land.

Throughout the scene Blum has been half asleep, unseeing, the absence of his caustic irony allowing his companion's fantasy to move unchecked. Georges's thinking returns of its own to the more immediate situation in Corinne's bed. Years

later, when a sober consideration of his surroundings forces
upon him more objective thoughts, he reflects on the anonymity
of the room where the "cold, unalterable and virginal mirror"
(42) that has captured the frenzy of a thousand loveless coup-
lings, opens into a multiplicity of dreams. The warmth and
languor emanating from Georges's vision of the young woman
finds in its center the prolific begetter of death-dealing armies;
the multiple encounters reflected by the mirror in the hotel
room are absorbed and frozen into its icy depths; the very
furniture of the room becomes the "dusty coffin of the reflected
ghosts of thousands of lovers" (42). Death prevails at the
core of desire. It soon calls forth a scene where the peasant
woman's brother threatens to shoot a man he suspects of
having seduced her. Metaphorical death has gained sufficient
substance to threaten a more factual manifestation.

The analogy with painting that introduced the barn sequence
anticipates reconstructions by Georges of the earlier suicide
of de Reixach's ancestor during the Convention period. In a
family portrait the paint altered by time has flowed from his
temple in a red stain. Elements of both visions, remembrance
of memories and imagination, are fused into another death-
generating infidelity. All realities, all dreams have the same
value in Georges's memory. With the evidence of Corinne
beside him, the memory of the farm girl and his speculations
about the ancestor's suicide in his mind, all distinctions lose
their meaning. Thus, the story of the deceived "Conventionnel"
becomes that of his deceived captain, and Georges, in a
supremely narcissistic gesture, assumes the role of all those
who made cuckolds of this venerable family from generation
to generation. As the novel progresses, the interpenetration
of death and love becomes more patent. The inventive assertive-
ness of language creates a direct narrative link between love
and death (*l'amour et la mort*), words predestined, it seems,
to remain together through sound and fused in the novel
through metaphor.

Georges's night with Corinne is rendered in detail only in
the third part of the book. This coitus, initiated in Part I and
completed in Part III, absent in the central portion, the origin
of Georges's remembrance, is also an accurate correlative of

the total development of the novel and an illustration of the meaning of the third epigraph. In order to join further the first and third sections in one indissoluble Love-Death duo, the vision which we examined earlier, whereby woman has become a central death-generating orifice, is pursued near the end of the second part and completed in the third. Hiding from a passing patrol Georges feels "as if he were trying to vanish between the lips of the ditch, to melt, to slip, to sink altogether through this narrow crevice to rejoin the original matter (matrix)" (249). The image is restated at the beginning of the last part where the metaphor becomes a tangible reality: "lying back there in the fragrant grass of the ditch in that furrow of the earth breathing smelling its black and bitter humus lapping her pink [thing]"[3] (261).

Georges's thoughts will now move constantly from his present with Corinne to his past in Flanders, from the metaphorical death of lovemaking to the clear danger of actual death in the retreat or the concentration camp. Dispersed and leaderless, Georges and his companions represent the last remnants of an army in dissolution, born of death-in-love, of the stylized vulva drawn by a soldier on a wall, his whole being concentrated on the point of a nail. Passion formalized, like accepted custom, is but an initiation to death.[4] In *The Flanders Road* the recurring image of a horse slowly sinking into the mud becomes the correlative of a world and a tradition in decay, the vast suicide of a nation.

III   *Eros and Tradition*

It is through its power to undermine such tradition that Eros exerts its only positive effect in *The Flanders Road*. De Reixach's decision to marry Corinne initiates the breakdown of those hereditary patterns which had been the framework of his life; this, together with her infidelity, renders his suicide at least a plausible alternative in Georges's mind. Concurrent to her lovemaking with Georges, Corinne's relationship with Iglésia is originally presented in the first segment of the novel, a consummated fact, as is de Reixach's reaction to it: "he had always pretended to notice nothing" (14). The comment is immediately followed in the text by some thoughts about this war in which proprieties have been ignored, form has become irrelevant—"where you were cut down before you had time to know it" (14)—intimating their consequential relation. The second part offers the details of Corinne's disruptive influence in de Reixach's life; her desirability as a woman, together with her capriciousness and refusal of convention, become the principal reasons for his welcoming death.

Corinne's is not a nature that accepts trodden ways. As opposed to other women of her class whose adolescent fragility changes without transition "into something rather masculine, rather horsey" (18), she seems bathed in timeless, elemental sexuality. She walks amid the formalized attire of the horserace crowd, "her vaporous and indecent red dress swaying, swirling around her legs—toward the grandstand" (23). In her appearance she epitomizes all that is the very opposite of her husband's manner: "the middleaged man, wry, dry, straight—and even still—impenetrable, and the girl of eighteen in her brilliant shameless gowns with that hair, that body, that skin" (59). Youth versus age, impenetrability versus unabashed openness, austerity versus lewdness, all are aspects of the basic antagonism between tradition and eroticism. Her body and her clothes, her flesh and her perfume are fused into one precious unreal unity toward the single purpose of seduction.

We perceive now that the previously negative import of Eros was but a result of the limitations imposed upon it by circumstance. It can also have the positive effect of breaking through the hereditary crust of convention, blurring the distinctions and the dialectic at the origin of war. Early in the novel, before the dissolving effect of Georges's Eros-centered recollection has begun its action, the very texture of time was armorlike, impervious: "... the air and time itself were only a single, solid mass of chilly steel..." (30). The soldiers are seized in this night as by metallic jaws. Their horses seem creaking legendary animals, "suggesting the image of some heraldic beast made not of flesh and muscles" (30).

Emblem of that social class which produces ministers and officers, the horse capsulizes their very way of life. Georges's memory, aided by the comments of Iglésia, delves into the circumstances of a particular horse-racing episode to illustrate the young woman's attack on the customs of her husband's world. As the latter insists on riding in a steeplechase—a ridiculous and uncalled-for display, she feels, aimed perhaps at impressing her—she instructs Inglésia to bet a large amount of money on the race. Her intention is to deny whatever elements of pride might remain in de Reixach's performance; she even refuses to know on whom the groom bets. In her eyes, the bet turns the race into a matter of money and stresses the uselessness of de Reixach's gesture.

The only detailed rendering of the squadron's initial disbanding is precisely introduced between two sequences devoted to the race, linking the episodes together, as if by their proximity a clearer light would fall on both. In this case, the instants that precede the machine-gun burst depict the squadron massive and intact. The shift from a traditional steeplechase to a war scene had to be from one formalized situation to another. And, in effect, for Georges the race is but the prelude to de Reixach's death. Near the finish line, the riders' appearance is a clear anticipation of a later time: "pathetic, absurd, the four horses exhausted, the four riders with their fish faces, mouths open and gasping for breath" (181–182).

Although Corinne had once asked de Reixach to buy horses for her, and had even intended to learn to ride, this whim soon passed; its only result is perhaps the lovemaking with Iglésia in the stable, another, more concrete attack on that world represented by the horse, that of the medieval knight, now a cavalry captain. Her role as de Reixach's wife is ambiguous in that she wants to belong to this social class and detests it at the same time, a state of mind parallel to that of Georges, whose decision to seduce her is certainly related to this feeling of kinship. Such an ambivalent attitude allows Corinne to fit particularly well the figure represented in an old print, whose description was discovered by Georges among the papers of the "Conventionnel." Several elements highlight the equivocal nature of this print; we read the translation, in eighteenth-century French, of an Italian description of a picture, some words remaining in the original. The subject of the print itself is somewhat ambiguous: it represents a

Centaur-woman embracing a young man, "who is embracing
her close while passing under this woman's right arm his own
left hand which emerges from under her shoulder. The young
man's gown is violet and the habit hanging from the arm
of the Centaurefs is yellow" (56).[5] The last lines of this text
are in Italian and point out the interdependence between the
centaurs, Bacchus and Venus. The situation is suggestive of a
reverse rendering of the Chiron and Aphrodite coupling, the
young man in the role of Aphrodite and the woman is that of
Chiron. The description of the garments worn by the couple
further underlines the ambivalence of the situation; owing to
the period to which both the print and the language belong,
the woman wears a "habit" (suit) and the man a "robe" (gown).

Earlier in this text, the horse half of the centaur-woman was
described as "light chestnut," the color of the filly ridden by
de Reixach in the race; in the torso and figure of the woman
"the eye distinguishes the delicacie of the white flesh-tintes"
(56), also Corinne's characteristic flesh tone; other terms in
the depiction have been elsewhere also applied to her.

Following this text, Georges relates for the first time the
story of the eighteenth-century de Reixach who shot himself
after a defeat by the Spaniards. Later developments of the
incident will gradually introduce imaginary escapades by the
ancestor's wife which would rank as equally convincing antecedents to the suicide. Pictures of this lady before and after
the suicide show her to have apparently gained by it, since
her later appearance is that of a more desirable woman,
sensuous and intriguing. In her role as the reverse of the mate
he might have hoped for, Corinne disrupts de Reixach's life
on all fronts. The ambivalence of her representation as a
centaur-woman is analogous to that of her actions, whereby
she adopts the standards of her class to destroy them, as
she destroys the husband she chooses. At the same time, the
description of the print suggests the disruptive action of unrestrained passion on the tenets of tradition by showing the
unexpected transformation of legend. The farm girl also, as
that particular incident is expanded, becomes the center of
an argument whose incestuous overtones bring to Georges's
mind the legendary Atrides. Hence, the wife of the "Conven-

tionnel," Corinne, and the farm girl all partake of the same primordial role as objects of desire, enemies of custom, and possible causes of death.

At the opposite pole of female antagonism, symbol of the conventions under its attack, the figure of the horse, both alive and dead, informs Georges's narrative with similar tenacity. It is the constant companion of Georges and his comrades' wanderings. The same mud-covered form of a dead horse[6] appears several times in the novel, point of departure and arrival of Georges' aimless meanderings after his squadron's rout. The circle traced and retraced by the soldiers around it is but a counterpart of the steeplechase circuit; such endless turning is characteristic of the formalized activity of the upper classes before the war, exemplified by de Reixach, of the irrelevant verbiage of intellectuals such as Georges's father,[7] of the repeated cycles of history gathered in the fiction. This apparition recurs with increasing frequency as the narrative progresses, the several descriptions paralleling stages of apparent disarray in which Georges's reconstruction would flounder. The first instance shows a horse already half-buried in the mud: "...something unexpected, unreal, hybrid, so that what had been a horse...was no longer anything now but a vague heap of limbs, of dead meat, of skin and sticky hair, three-quarters covered with mud..." (25). The description continues for more than two pages, concluding with Georges's rotating movement around this central object, an anticipation of the vaster circling to ensue, and a metaphor for the growth of the narrative itself: "the outlines continually changing, in other words that kind of simultaneous destruction and reconstruction of lines and volumes" (28). Midway in this passage a bright-red stain of blood stands out on the brown and black background of mud.

Together with numerous references, the narrative contains two more detailed depictions of the same animal, the second one linking Parts I and II, the third one near the end of Part II; they show significant variations as well as some recurring elements. The hardness imperiled by liquefaction which appeared in the first instance becomes later fragile and earth-like, as if in a second stage of digestion by the earth only

the more stubborn elements resisted, their substance already
absorbed. The blood has turned a dark brown, reminiscent of
the stain in the portrait of de Reixach's ancestor. The circling
is now that of the sun. The last description shows the horse
almost totally assimilated by the earth and Georges seeing it
at ground level; the terminology is now more general, and
historical comparisons are established with legendary horses
of the past. Georges himself, flattened against the dirt, feels
as if he were dissolving into it, slowly rotting. The turning
wheels of military trucks expand the concept of circularity
to suggest that of the entire war and that of history, initiated
by the previous comparisons with mythical steeds. Georges
is now alone, in his moment of greatest danger.

The progressive disappearance of this animal illustrates the
idea of breakdown on several levels: (1) that of Georges's
squadron; (2) that of de Reixach's world; (3) that of the
nation. The historical and legendary comparisons, together
with the second implication of circularity (the sun), reintroduce the conflict between Eros and tradition (ancestor, and
woman as the perennial threat), and reinforce the notion of
its inevitability. Finally, Georges's own fear of death, his position flat against the ground, which will occasion his return
to the present and Corinne's arms, and the circular motion of
the truck wheels suggest again the total development of his
recollection as the interaction of Eros, death, and convention.

IV *Eros and Memory*

Georges's whole effort of remembrance has been itself a
struggle against the liquefying action of time. Mud, as the
raw material of life, imposes its nauseating presence throughout the novel. It transforms and dissolves, sometimes producing
life, but a symbol always of disintegration and death. It is
the earth melting and reabsorbing her own. As he tries to hide,
Georges wants once more to become a fetus, to return to his
mother's womb, and then finds himself making love to Corinne.
At other times, riding in the night, the rain, earth, and sky
seem to become a primordial matter in which Georges slowly
dissolves.

His memory functions as a mirror wherein are reflected with equal clarity his dreams and his recollections. The narrative is the result of this reflection. Memory resists the tyranny of duration; its time has no more reality than the images it reflects; it is indivisible, an eternal present, the only one that truly exists for Georges: "the progress of time itself, that is, invisible immaterial with neither beginning nor end nor point of reference" (29). In this universe devoid of intrinsic reality, where causality resides in words more than in their object, comprehension is possible only through superimposed images in the mirror of language. And as a reflected vision can disappear with flashing speed, so will time be projected beyond its measurable limits. Angle of vision and temporal point of view are synonymous.

It is possible to discern four different chronological periods in the novel, though they invariably merge with one another: (1) Georges and Blum's reconstruction of the story of the Conventionnel, based on Georges's vague memories of childhood dreams, disparate heirlooms, fragments of Sabine's stories, and his imagination; (2) the investigation of the antecedents of de Reixach's "suicide": moments of the latter's married life, based on Iglésia's reports and Georges's own meager knowledge; (3) Georges's memories of his wanderings during the retreat, of his journey to the concentration camp, and of his conversations there with Blum or Iglésia, wherein were recalled the elements of (1) and (2); (4) A present-past, his night with Corinne, during which he recalls everything, rendered in the past tense. The effect of this fusion of imagined and real past is to diminish the general degree of factuality of true memories, because of a disproportionate importance given to the hypothetical. Indeed, the night spent with Corinne, while it is the only immediate experience in the novel, seems no more real than the remotest remembrance or the most conjectural speculation.

Within this gallery of mirrors, where reality loses its substance through countless reflections, the visual mode will predominate. Georges engages in a constant effort to photograph his memories, as it were, or to conceive of scenes as paintings, their immobility lending itself more readily to analysis. The result is a series of fixed moments, within the flow of narration, whose components disintegrate immediately Georges's attention relaxes. Such occasions become narrative vortices where static description seems to shift irrevocably toward movement under the momentum of the protagonist's imagination. His need to see precedes his need to understand; it will be the scenes that he has not himself witnessed, those that are either reported to him by Iglésia, for instance, or that he simply imagines, that he will try hardest to anchor down. Thus, from Iglésia's comments on the steeplechase arises one of the most striking frozen sequences in the novel: "And again it was as if I were seeing it: silhouetted against the deep, almost blackish green of the opulent chestnut trees, the jockeys passing ... like this: Yellow, blue suspenders and cap—the blackish-green background of the chestnut trees—Black, blue St. Andrew's cross and white cap—the blackish-green wall of the chestnut trees—Blue-and-pink check, blue cap—the blackish-green wall of the chestnut trees ..." (21). And so on, through almost an entire page. Movement soon disrupts this stability, allowing the penetration of metaphors, transforming imagined objectivity into poetic consideration; near the end of the passage the fillies seem to be "dancing, seeming to be suspended above the earth, without touching ground" (22). The initial precision soon is eroded by figurative language.

It is here that we perceive the function in the narrative of the present participle, the tense most adequate to render images as fixed moments within mobility. By describing a movement that has neither end nor beginning, the present participle detains the temporal flow and isolates instants in an unassailable present. Furthermore, it offers the isolated action, frozen in its evolution, without antecedents or results, that is at the basis of the novel. Moments when action is arrested are also those when present participles are most frequent, where incident is manifestly delivered from time. Such moments frequently reveal the conjunction of love and death, in prolonged forceful commentaries to the epigraph by Malcolm de Chazal. Such is the instant leading to the discovery of the ancestor's body: two servants rush into the room, one of them a maid holding a candle "which she is trying to protect from the draft caused by the bursting open of the door (the gleam of the flame passing . . .) holding at the same time in one hand that shift . . . and the candle she is protecting with the other" (87). As the scene proceeds, the present participles increase, the description becoming more and more that of a print showing explosive but arrested movement.

This sequence and that of the farm girl (see above) are the subject of repeated amplifications, transformations, and adjustments. Their erotic connotations become in Georges's mind (and that of Blum, his alter ego) a basis for their equivalence as sources of speculation, and then for their merging. Thus, Georges will retain his vision of the young woman at the barn door as a painting, the origin of his memories of the Convention ancestor, and see the maid rushing to the ancestor's door bathed in the same light that illuminated the farm girl's face. As vessels of the same erotic and death-generating potential, all women are interchangeable, as are all their representations.

V   *Eros and Language*

The scene pictured by Georges, where the servants discover the body of de Reixach's ancestor, manifests a gradual shift in descriptive emphasis from the subject (the print) to the execution itself. Already in the initial stages, the text underlines the idea of representation: there is an abundance of verbs and substantives pertaining to the act of recounting—"spoken of only in hushed tones," "Sabine said," "had always told her," "a legend, a piece of slander, scandal spread by the servants," and so on (86)—until a transitional phrase introduces the narrator's own elaboration: "something in the style of one of those prints called The Surprised Lover or The Seduction" (87). The descriptions of the two main figures in the print move imperceptibly from their form and movement to their manner of representation. The actions suggested by the stance of the maid—"stifle a scream," "clumsily holding together the garment," "which she is trying to protect" (87)—give place gradually to considerations of lines, shadows and volumes— "the shadows reversed . . . placed not beneath the masses but above them, the parts in darkness being the lower lip, the ridge of the nose" (87–88). The form of the valet follows a similar pattern until the drawing instrument itself and the technique become central concerns: "the shadow which the engraving needle indicated by fine crosshatchings" (88). The corpse of the Conventionnel is relegated to the very end of the passage and rendered exclusively in terms of the light it absorbs.

In this conjunction of two forms of representation, the paramount importance of language at the foundation of circumstance is revealed. The print is one of those which "tell a story" with, at its bottom a "legend," a hybrid representation midway between narrative and plastic design. Furthermore, as opposed to the portrait of the Conventionnel, a "true" memory, this scene is pure surmise, verbal invention. Lastly, the gradual transfer of focus in the description from the fictional element to the means and manner of design suggests again the paramount importance of the latter—"lines," "volumes," "engraving needle" translate into "words"; only language remains. The pattern of this passage corresponds to the condition of the entire narrative. Anecdotal and linguistic incident are fused, and the activity of language becomes the underlying plot. In this sense, discord will remain at the very heart of the reconstruction, undermining it from within, actualizing the rift within the recording consciousness as it expresses it. Hence it is while it depicts the disruptive penetration of uncontainable Eros that language most clearly displays its power as an autonomous force.

From the very beginning Corinne appears as a source of dissension. She is at the origin of the whole narrative, the occasion for Georges to come face to face with the unresolved ambivalence of his thinking. As we earlier saw, she is introduced by means of parenthetical statements that underline her ambiguous role. These statements appear as wedges inserted in the otherwise compact flow of language; they are destined to increase in importance, precluding any possibility of fusion. The parenthesis itself can be seen both as the form taken by incidental comment, and as a more general statement on the composition of the novel. In effect, the three parts of the narrative could be conceived as the three elements of a parenthesis. The first and third part contain some indications about the present of narration (through Corinne's presence), while the central one concerns less "real" events (farther in the past, generally, or more imaginary). It is also an accurate picture of Georges's inner disjunction, the fissure he wants to weld by relegating the present moments with Corinne to the past, thus joining the woman's ongoing adultery to the antecedents of de Reixach's death. He would then assume the role of final, complete cuckolder of the captain, provide a reason for the latter's willingness to die, make his suicide all the more plausible. At the same time he would exorcise his past and meet squarely his present condition.

This cannot be accomplished while Corinne remains with him; she continues to be a vortex of disruption, imbuing all the other female figures with the same power, and creating a pattern of increasing fragmentation wherein the only effective links are those established by language divorced from time. A consideration of the earliest parenthetical statements is indicative of this very tendency toward dispersion. The very first parenthesis, a short one, relates to the effect of Sabine's letter on de Reixach and points to the variance between his feelings and the demands of convention. This idea is restated and amplified in the following ones pertaining to Corinne, since she represents both an expression of his passion and an attack on his way of life. The parentheses grow in length and complication as the narrative proceeds, all referring to ideas related to fragmentation, either directly or metaphorically.

The narrative point of view itself underlines the concept of a bisected vision. The novel begins and ends as a first person narrative, but the larger part of it is in the third person. The shift from first person to third person occurs upon the first description of the dead horse, that from third back to first at the beginning of the last part. There is no gain in objectivity when the narrative appears in the third person, simply a further distinction drawn in the quality of remembrance: the first-person memory is a direct one; the third-person memory suggests a greater distance, since it interposes the narrator between the reader and the text. This scheme also divides the text into three main parts: The first part to page 29 establishes its principal elements in Georges's first-person recall from Corinne's arms. Upon meeting with the dead horse in his memories of Flanders, Georges's recollection changes to the third person; his "present" situation is almost totally drowned in the flow of the past, where the narrator sees himself impersonally, where he remembers himself recalling and re-creating events or scenes from other times, and where temporal distinctions become fluid; as a third person narrative within a first person remembrance, it is free of the anchor to the "present" that "I" signifies. This mode remains until the third part of the novel, where once more, as the first person narrative resumes, the immediacy of Georges's embrace with Corinne takes over and his memories are interspersed with prolonged descriptions of lovemaking.

Georges is conscious throughout of the transformation that the narrative effectuates upon his memory. It is a concerted effort to transform likelihood into legend, sordidness into drama. Blum, who has assumed the sarcastic voice in the relation, aptly and succinctly summarizes its value: "... you're always sifting, supposing, embroidering, inventing fairy tales where I bet no one except you has never seen anything but an everyday piece of sex between a whore and two fools..." (187). Corinne, as the confidante of large portions of the tale, also understands Georges's endeavors, a purely selfish effort to resolve the ambivalence within himself; she understands that she is herself nothing but the instrument of his reordering of the past; that she means nothing else to him. She leaves him, furious at having been abused more deeply than ever before.

At this point Georges begins to question the value of his enterprise, comparing it to his father's own work, realizing how he has himself fallen into the trap of believing that words can provide solutions: "... perhaps it was as futile, as senseless as unreal as to make hentracks on sheets of paper and to look for reality in words..." (301). De Reixach's death continues to haunt him; the present rushes in: "... what time do you think it is...?" (302), but this question is immediately applied to that previous event, and a new recapitulation begins. Georges's last effort is one of objectivity. He returns to statements at the beginning of the novel where lack of sleep distorted his vision. He tries to think now of his wanderings in Flanders in terms of a map, listing the points they traveled through in a column of names.

The disposition of these names along the page itself transmits the effort to transform a circular path into a straight line.[8] This arrangement corresponds in the structure to the rendering of the translated page from the manuscript of de Reixach's ancestor: it represents an endeavor to recall an exact terminology, while underlining the attempt to "straighten out" the circle. In effect, considering that earlier passage to be a description of Corinne and all she represents as *femme-centaure,* we understand the disintegrating form of the dead horse to be its own counterpart. As the remembered wanderings return inevitably to that shape, so does the narrative proceed from and towards Corinne. Thus, both circularities are resolved into that of the broader linguistic circularity of the novel. Its last moments then become a summarized restatement of the whole. They begin as an effort to visualize the battle as on a war map. The description continues with an emphasis on the external, military aspect of events; the soldiers are described in terms of their equipment, with details of weight and utility. The horses become animals of war, their wounds seen as simple impairments to their efficiency: "the animals not having been unsaddled for six days and probably having bad saddle sores caused by friction and lack of air" (308). Yet we already note here the creeping uncertainty ("probably").

In spite of the effort to return only to probable facts, the narrative is plunged once more into contingency, and once more the question, "but how can you tell, how can you tell?" (308) returns to haunt Georges. Inevitably the attempt to understand again transforms likelihood into sheer surmise. Distances and times are furnished, but they do not help. This coordinating of emptied-out events on the map of his memory, while it deprives them of their emotional content does not produce further understanding. Exasperation and despair return as Georges discards the central image of the narrative: ". . . one last time I saw it I had time to recognize it thinking that now it must have begun stinking for good oh fine let it rot where it lies let it infect fester until the whole earth the whole world is forced to hold its nose..." (314).

The use of "last time" applies almost exclusively to what the vision has all along represented, a moment in the narrative, the center of an activity now ending. Following this, the former obsession with metaphor, detail, and supposition returns, still dominated by the figure of de Reixach. Language begins anew to assume the autonomy it had for a moment lost, with echoes of the opening of the novel. But, whereas the basic elusiveness of words was then introduced in the manner of parenthetical puns pertaining to Corinne, here the center of the narration and the source of its fluidity is indirectly acknowledged to be Georges. He becomes the subject of the last pun of the novel.[9] The cycle has once more begun. A rapid rerun of the initial patterns takes place: death of de Reixach, death of the Conventionnel, questions about both confused in their "suicide," a dying horse. It is a final effort to allow words to conclude, to use up their material, as it were. But the questions remain: "But did I really see him or think I saw him or merely imagine him afterwards or even only dream it all..." (320). The narrative ends as it consciously abandons the decaying world it brought forth, "the world stopped frozen crumbling...left to the incoherent, casual, impersonal and destructive work of time." (320).

CHAPTER 4

The Palace: *Death's Progress*

I *Introduction*

S IMON'S investigation of man's encounter with death, a
crucial aspect of the novels so far examined, becomes in
The Palace the very underpinning of the narrative's composition. Once more, we witness the recollection of a narrator whose
past proximity with death has scarred his consciousness and
left within him an irreparable fissure. Recalling those circumstances he tries to fathom their every facet, hopeful that
language can elucidate that portion of his past.

As in *The Flanders Road* the situation is one of violence,
though it appears here in potential rather than fact, the narrator
aware merely of its antecedents, or its repercussions. No specific
historical facts are offered, but the setting of the novel appears
to be a Spanish coastal city on the Mediterranean, Barcelona
probably; the time is the Civil War (1936–1939).

The memories are occasioned by the narrator's return to the
city fifteen years later. His recall is given in the third person
and centers around the activities he witnessed. Although he
was a foreigner and a student, he had gained admittance to
the headquarters of a revolutionary group in a luxurious hotel,
the Palace, now transformed into a political and administrative
center.

In its spareness, the action itself is more reminiscent of
The Grass than of *The Flanders Road*. It spans a period of
three days during the revolution,[1] interrupted occasionally by
rapid shifts to the moments of remembrance fifteen years later.
These transitions become more frequent at the conclusion of
the novel, the last lines appearing in the present, the narrator
now hopelessly confined to his immediate spatiotemporal limits.

In a room of the Palace the student and four men comment

73

on the recent murder of a revolutionary hero. One of them, an American, views the incident as a symptom of the failure of the revolution and seems to blame, though not overtly, the individuals there present, or the organization they represent. Through a series of metaphors the narrator's memory shifts to the preceding night when he arrived at the city by train. An Italian, the "Rifle," now present also, detailed to him the manner in which at some previous time he had shot a man, also Italian, in a Paris restaurant. His story continues after the train stops, as he and the student are driven at reckless speed from the station to their quarters in the city. We then return to the room at the Palace, from whose window the men watch the funeral procession of Santiago, the assassinated hero.

The American's sarcastic comments continue later as he, the student, the Italian, and a vaguely official-looking companion sit at a sidewalk cafe that same evening. The discussion between the American and the uniformed man is on the verge of becoming dangerously hostile when the Italian suggests they all go to bed; the student and the American are to meet the next day. In his room the student is unable to sleep; he feels that the American is in some peril and debates whether he should call on him. He is awakened in the middle of the night by the noise of someone running and of slammed car doors. The next day the American does not come to the rendezvous at the cafe. The student runs to the Palace to inquire. After being barred access to the building (there has been a change in the identification papers), he finally rushes in, taking advantage of the confusion caused by a sudden cloudburst, and reenters the room where they had all met before. There he is told that no one knows where his friend is. As he leaves, he sees the "officer," who says that the American has left for the front.

The student returns to the café. At this point, the present begins to intrude with greater force. He thinks he recognizes the Italian walking across the square in the crowd. He runs after him uselessly; finally he goes down into a public lavatory where past and present meet as he vomits, seeing the shoeshiners' boxes as children's coffins, relics of the revolution and his dead past.

The epigraph chosen by Simon to head the novel is the first Larousse definition of the word *Revolution*: "Revolution: the locus of a moving body which, describing a closed curve, successively passes through the same points." Most notable in the choice of this particular description, in light of the novel's setting, is its limitation to movement and form. Historical and political meanings are ignored, and the reader is directed to the most objective and abstract sense of the term. Three main factors appear necessary for a revolution: a moving object, circularity, and repetition. Considering the close correlation previously exhibited by Simon's epigraphs with the general composition of his novels, an examination of these three ideas with relation to *The Palace* should prove fruitful.

The origin and end of the novel's movement, the points along its circularity, all contain death or reflect it. The situation itself is pervaded by deaths past and deaths to come. The narrator's self-imposed task is to understand now this fated past, in a reenumeration that is itself a repetition, a re-creation through language of events that remained mysterious in all but their connotations. Caught in the inexorable onrush of that particular fragment of history, the erstwhile student feels betrayed, in-effectual, and somehow guilty. His present effort to reexamine those days limned by death is also meant to exorcise through understanding and words, as is the Simon protagonist's wont, the condemnation that weighs upon him from that time. In his endeavor, the narrator will proceed from the relative certainty and innocence of the beginning, through increasing doubt, to the final realization of an irreconcilable disjunction, where the past is neither solved nor dispensable, but reaches into the present to wound it. In this novel also, imagination overcomes and transforms remembered fact. Metaphor moves beyond its role as expansive of meaning to acquire a life of its own, creating new directions for the text, incorporating the nimbus of death, to become itself ultimately a deadly threat to the narrator.

The novel comprises five titled chapters. Its development follows the rising dominance of death and death-related ideas through three gradations: (1) Death represented within the fiction: There are depictions of death as a pervading menace (chapter 1, "Inventory," the death of the revolution, the murder of Santiago), and the account of one particular assassination by the Rifle (chapter 2, "The Rifle's Story"). In both cases, the idea of representation, the translation of events into words or pictures, dominates. The death of Santiago is given in terms of newspaper headlines; the Italian himself recounts his act to the student with the assistance of a diagram. Near the end of this chapter, the student is placed in closer proximity to danger during the nightmarish drive into the city, anticipating the second step in the ascent. (2) Death Witnessed: Two chapters constitute the two moments of this sequence. In chapter 3, "The Funeral of Patroclus," the populace in Santiago's funeral procession is described in metaphors that underline its contained violence, vaguely directed at the Palace and particularly at the men watching from the balcony. Chapter 4, "In the Night," follows the student's own implication, through his passivity, in the possible murder of the American, and his anguished, sleepless night. (3) Death Endured: The last chapter, "Lost and Found," brings together the strands introduced in "Inventory" and developed as far as chapter 4; the student now feels in danger, factually at first, because of his acquaintance with the American and the changes in revolutionary policy that he now suspects; figuratively later, this time in a more intimate, less avoidable manner, as the recalled, reinvented past reaches into his present and negates it. Our inquiry will attempt to follow these three stages of death's advance with particular emphasis on the interplay of metaphor and recollection, and the undermining of present awareness and certainty by remembrance.

II *Entry*

In a descriptive movement reminiscent of that which introduced the decaying horse in *The Flanders Road*, the first lines of *The Palace* focus upon the sudden appearance of a pigeon on a balcony. The bird is introduced as "it," and only through inference and a parenthetical comparison, after some lines of text, do we understand that "it" is a pigeon. The immediacy of the bird's presence precedes any thought of identification and the importance of its exact nature appears secondary to its movement. A notable feature of the pigeon is its unexpected size; it seems enormous "probably because you always see them from a distance."[2] It is described mainly in terms of hardness: "like a porcelain dove," "[glints of emerald],"[3] "coppery," "coral feet," (14). Another incongruity related to its size is its plumpness in a hungry city, the narrator asking himself why it has not been caught and eaten. Its movements are short and imperceptible; the bird appeared as if "materialized by a magician's wand" (13), and it disappears with equal suddenness, probably because someone moved inside.

The very introduction of the bird by the unspecific "it" bears a number of consequences with regard to the text: it assumes a later role therein for the bird, anticipates the development of the role, and instructs the reader as to the significance of the bird by suggesting that it need not be named, that the text will undertake to identify it clearly; therefore, the writing itself is emphasized at the expense of the object it describes; it underlines movement and presence as opposed again to identity, and thereby also directs our attention to the representation as such. All these elements immediately illustrate the connotations of the epigraph, indicate the direction of the narrative and propose that of our attention.

Already we see the tendency of language to impart movement and change to an unchanging object. Pigeons, in effect, and the shell of the Palace itself, will remain static in the novel among those objects that will survive; albeit the Palace, as more particularly manmade, will undergo some transformations. Language will ceaselessly attack these elements, trying to include them in its death-generating march. They are brought together in one of the last visions of the novel with the flapping of the birds' flight an ironic comment on the concluding adventure: "the rustling flight of pigeons passing again for the second time, circling and applauding in front of the façade of the Palace" (250). Pigeon and Palace partake of the same nature; palaces such as the one in question will remain as long as they are needed by the wealthy. They too, like pigeons, are interchangeable. As points of departure of the fiction, the durability of both components makes them allies of death's progress, for what the text cannot transform and destroy it will assimilate. They become the pervasive witnesses of the narrator's growing anguish. They both become also emblems of the failure which the narration details: the Palace is an epitome of the reason for the revolution; feeding the pigeons is the activity left to old men whose revolution failed and who survive in resignation. Likewise, the pigeons' circular flight becomes a correlative of history's circularity, and so does the changing of the Palace's furniture, imagined by the narrator as a double line of men climbing and descending the spiral staircase, one laden with objects of luxury, the other with utilitarian ones.

The introduction of these two items is followed by an inventory of the furniture and objects now in the Palace's room, "between the four paneled and *dove-gray* walls" (italics mine) (17), where the student is. The last objects are two pictures, tacked to the walls, of two unidentified men whose description suggests Marx and Stalin, as well as a map of the city. Until this last element, the objects described offer the text no opening, no possibility of development save toward the past. Those whose past use suggests a history are depicted in terms of their previous avatars. Those too plain, whose utility is obviously restricted (a small office table, a wooden rocking chair, a kitchen chair) are bypassed. The two pictures are pointedly ignored (we know who the men are) as closed representations, flat pictorial surfaces that allow no access, whose significance is already patent. All these items are inside the room, but no attention is paid to their positions. Only the map of the city is exactly situated and offers obvious openings to writing: "on the panel left of the window (above the little desk with the typewriter, set diagonally in the corner of the room) a plan of the city with its blocks of houses shown in yellow, its streets drawn in a regular grid"[4] (20). The text will enter this inviting, open frame and develop therefrom.

Ingress is achieved by means of a parenthesis and suggests the funnellike movement of the prose, its penetration into a flat surface animating the dead squares of the city. The importance of the representation and its autonomous development is further underlined by the fact that the text finds its entrance also through a representation. It is a skeletal picture of the city that language is to fill out, paradoxically giving it life in order to transform it into the setting of multiform death.

III   *Death Represented*

The parenthetical entry toward the central activity of the fiction is also the first dialogue of the novel and links the city map, last object of the "inventory," with the initial unspecified pervasiveness of death: "('. . . like a sewer grating,' the American said, 'and if you lifted it up you'd find underneath the corpse of a stillborn child wrapped in old newspapers . . .')" (20–21). These remarks, later elaborated by the American, already suggest a first stage of development. They usher in the initial mystery, the murder of Santiago, as a symptom of illness of the newborn revolution. We still only learn of the assassination through newspaper headlines. These also anticipate the second mystery: the American's own disappearance in the night.

The connection between the ailing revolution and the murdered hero is specified further on; the corpse is "Victim of the preinfantile disease of the revolution" (21). The relationship between words and death is intimated by a first metaphor ("wrapped in old newspapers") and more directly stated shortly after: "thrown into the sewers in a shroud of words . . . strangled by the umbilical cord of miles of enthusiastic phrases" (21). The danger run by the American himself is implied by the disapproval with which his remarks are received: he is repeatedly told to keep quiet.

At the close of the parenthesis the description of the city is pursued, now installing the student as the central consciousness of the narrative. His vision continues to unite the dying revolution with the dying city, while the same metaphor announces the funeral of the assassinated hero, and reaches back to enclose the history of the nation: "the somber and overwhelming perspectives of streets, squares and avenues named after kings, saints, dogmas, battles; barbaric and flowery, like a horrible catafalque, like a dead woman on a bed of rose petals . . ." (22–23). The list of street names that follows offers a visual representation of this straight delving into the past, a progression contrasting with the parenthetical statement

where the circularity of the "present" was underlined: there
was a constant repetition and elaboration of the same thoughts
by the American, his actions themselves suggesting this movement "slipping the clip into the stock of his enormous revolver"
(21). Revolver and revolution are words akin in the violence
they contain, the movement they suggest, and their very written
form.

The circularity of remembered events finds its counterpart
in the continuing circularity in death of the present of remembrance. The student, years later, seated at a bar, sees himself
then, "that residue of himself, or rather that trace, that stain
(that excrement, so to speak) left behind himself" (24–25).
His superior, mocking stance is not sufficient, however, and
already the text introduces into this seemingly isolated moment
a metaphorical dimension that links it inexorably to the past.
The air of death and sterility has remained. The plentifulness
of food displayed in the bar, though it seems the very opposite
of that wartime scarcity, is touched by death, "like those pro-
visions laid in tombs for the nourishment of the dead" (27).
The waiter seems "a soldier drilling" (27), and inevitably there
remain "the same smell, the same stench of rancid oil and
public lavatories, . . . the same square, . . . the same pot-bellied
pigeons" (27).

The movement toward the unfolding recollection of the
newspapers and their headlines is gradual. The text, as it
appears to grope for the exact memory, turns attention upon
itself by describing first in a parenthesis the activity of the
reader, rather than the material read. This emphasis on the
events surrounding reading as an action also, by extension,
affects the depiction as such. What the headline offers in effect
is the first *representation* of death, capitals standing out in the
middle of the page. It grows tentatively. First an incomplete
question, the spelling itself mistaken, affected by the student's
native French, it then becomes a clear statement. Other captions
continue to the end of the chapter, all relating the same event.
A struggle ensues, characteristic of the development of the
whole novel, wherein the narrator is confronted by the growing
autonomous power of his own narrative, here centering around
the self-generated impetus of the headlines. To deflect attention

again, he focuses on the activities of the other men in the room, and the shape of the capital lettering of a banner. Both, however, point back to the center: the discussion concerns the murder, the inscription on the banner is *Trabajadores* ("workers") and directs us to the murder of their champion.

As the intrusive titles become clearer, their meaning more specific, the student retreats into a vaster questioning of the accuracy of the whole episode, taking temporary refuge in the now of remembrance: "... perhaps nothing had ever happened..." (36). Such refusal of the mystery tries to minimize the threat posed by memory, forcibly encasing it in a safely isolated past, relegating it to ironic obsolescence: "standing there... slightly unreal, slightly out of date, among the chubby ghosts of the tumbled chambermaids and the surprised bather" (39). But the march of language is overwhelming. Concurrent with a sudden explosion of questioning headlines, the American's comments reach their apex of sarcasm and specific accusation. The responses they elicit from the "schoolteacher," the individual who seems here to be in charge, are ominous in their calm disapproval. The danger menacing the American is but a reflection of the student's own precarious position, then, as his friend, and now, in the act of remembering.

As the narrative veers toward the general interchangeable attitude and appearance of men such as the schoolteacher, their indestructible, fanatical devotion to the cause, a long parenthesis introduces a memory of similar men seen by the narrator from a train. On the suitcase of one of them is a recognizable signature. This common name, *Jesús Nicolás Hernández*, in ornate longhand, is the response to the previous headlines and particularly to the one stating "The Crime has been signed"[5]: the implication is that it was committed by one of these permutable individuals, any one of them, for their struggle. Significantly, it is at a point when the text is becoming ever more autonomous, when its own impetus is carrying it forward in a headlong rush, that we are offered at the level of calligraphic correspondence a solution to the first death-related mystery of the novel. The parenthetical disposition of this sequence at the end of chapter 1 functions as a deeper funneling in of the text within that which earlier initiated the fictional sequence; it marks a further penetration into the world of simile and metaphor,[6] a further liberation of the language.

As he comments on the indestructibility of such individuals as the schoolteacher, and their pervasiveness, the example of men seen in a train station soon turns into a particular sequence wherein the student found himself involved; the events also become gradually more specific and lead the narrative to "The Rifle's Story." The unstoppable momentum of words finds here its correlative in the train journey during which this relation takes place. To the narrative funneling, the movement of language towards greater self-assertiveness, corresponds a temporal one: the Italian narrates an incident that took place years before.

Four levels of increasing linguistic autonomy are now definable: (1) penetration of language into the map of the city through the parenthesis leading to (2) the ascendency gained by the mystery of the headlines (another example of the ability of words both to reveal and veil events), leading to (3) a further penetration of language through another parenthesis, into a sequence of its own design (men in station), leading to (4) another level of narration, now thoroughly beyond the narrator's control, the Italian's story.

In terms of time sequences we have in a parallel movement: From (1) the remembrance of the situation in the Palace (men, room, conversation), to (2) headlines relating to an event accomplished in the immediate past, to (3) the train journey belonging to a yet previous moment, to (4) the Italian's story referring to a more remote period, years before.

As we pointed out above, the train journey accompanying (3) and (4) in both series effectively suggests the impetus acquired by language. To further stress this point, the last lines of the chapter become the first lines of the following one, the break standing out as a superimposed division upon an ongoing flow of prose. This pattern will be pursued subsequently[7] to accentuate the necessary artifice of the whole composition.

Death is still now at an early stage of its progress, the narrative viewing it in terms of secondary representations (headlines); but the "student's" control over the narrative has significantly diminished: this is the Italian's own account. In an effort parallel to that surrounding the headlines on Santiago's murder, he tries continuously to mitigate the impact of the Rifle's relation through his own incidental comments. These efforts appear first as a wish to know the exact nature of the objects described by the Italian, or through elaborate hypotheses about the man's friends and their life as underground political activists. He is in effect trying to defuse, as it were, the potential violence of the story, make its language his own, diminish its threat. Even his renditions, however, inevitably diverge toward violence and death, and he must then question the basic reasons for the confidence: "But why is he telling me all this?" (65).

When the Italian begins to trace a plan as an aid to his story, the narrator's attention is directed to the superficial aspects of this procedure: the quality of the paper, the Italian's concentration, his handling of the pencil. Again the very description of the pencil lines allows the metaphor to introduce an anticipation of the central incident: "lines ... that dug into the smudged paper like furrows of a metallic shiny leaden gray" (67).[8] Once more, death is present in even the most external details of representation. As the moment of the murder approaches in the Italian's story, the student's own recoiling from it, his attempt to refuse it or minimize it, become more transparent. He tries to fill the Italian's drawing with his own diminishing interpretation of the event, comparing the action to a game of war played on paper by classroom dunces. The transformation, however, contains visible within it the elements of its own disintegration; parenthetical statements break up its continuity, contrasting their movement with its fixity. After this initial rendition of the central event, the text will approach it and restate it through an accumulation of representational effects, arrogating to itself the *activity* of the event it describes and depriving the occurrence of its impact.[9]

The development begins as the Rifle sees himself entering the restaurant and struggling against his own reflection on the glass panes of the revolving door. The transition between himself and the sketch he is using is accomplished by means of a neon arrow from an outside advertisement reflected upon the door; an arrow represents his own movement also on the sketch. The representation suffers its initial division: The Rifle, remembering his action, sees his reflection on the door, and the arrow reflected on the door becomes his movement as an arrow on the sketch.

The participants in the incident will now undergo a series of transformations subject to the various modes of representation of the shooting that the narrative undertakes. They first partake of a double identity both as elements in the Rifle's drawing and in his memory. They are organized in terms of movement, light, and color circulating around the intruder. This is followed by an effort to visualize the motions and color of the scene in terms of a painting, a process that returns to the scheme of the first chapter and undertakes to present the elements in the field of vision as an ordered sequence: firstly, secondly, etc. A woman's scream reintroduces confusion into this temporary stasis and the final "take" of the scene returns to mobility by the intermediary of the Rifle's own confused thinking. At this point, the accumulation of minute impressions and surmises imbues the spectacle with the inexorable momentum of a slow-motion film, the revolver jumping at the end of the killer's hand, a simple continuation of all this movement from which he is himself separated: "the heavy-caliber revolver trembling then, beginning to make a series of violent leaps in his own hand" (84).

Here the student's mind once more intervenes, "But why is he telling me all this" (85), attempting an objective view, restructuring the event as a more intellectually acceptable one, trying to dampen its violence: "...wondering what it was that impelled a man to tell his story ('Or to tell his story to himself,' he thought: ...that is, to reconstruct, to reconstitute by means of verbal equivalents something he had seen or done...)" (85). Again his words have reached beyond their intended application to refer to himself and the character of the very enterpise he is embarked on, the whole narrative, preparing his own future guilt and vulnerability.

To underline the intrinsic power of the depiction as such, relative to that of the event, the scene has sustained a series of mutations, which, while they effectively transmit the chaotic nature of the incident, translate the action to the sphere of representation: that is to say, the action becomes a multiplicity, an accumulation of representational modes. The net effect is to slow down the "real" events toward fixity, while the movement is assumed by the description. There are three general renditions of the totality of the occurrence: (1) The narrator's own anticipation of the action; (2) The killer's confused experience; (3) The narrator's evaluation in terms of the reasons for the killer's relation. To those overviews correspond several forms of expression applied to various segments of the complete sequence; the main ones are: (1) The initial breakup of the scene into hybrid elements belonging to the sketch and the actual identity of the participants; (2) The vision in terms of movement, light, and color; (3) The subsequent more ordered arrangement, an inventory, as of masses of color in a painting.

Inevitably, death comes ever closer to the narrator. As he and the Italian are driven through the city by an apparently demented driver, the killer impassively continues his tale. A sudden turn throws him against the student, who feels "the gun barrel that stuck into his ribs, and the Italian's fragile body that weighed almost a ton crushing him in the corner of the seat" (90). It is as if the whole weight of the man's past, of his actions, were directly set on the shoulders of his companion. In an effort to escape the continuing, repetitive tale, the student, noticing a passing statue (probably Columbus)[10] imagines the spread of Spanish civilization over the world. Once more, a list of names of cities provides a column whereby entry can be gained into linear time. The idea of representation once more offers an apparent exit, as the text proceeds from the statue to its appearance on postage stamps, to the founding of cities. The Italian's voice, however, intrudes irresistibly, cutting through the student's effort to apply elsewhere his thought. Restricted now to this present, he turns to the city he is in, where death and destruction reign.

Bursting out of the restaurant, the Italian sees the same scene he had noticed before he went in, a man paying a taxi driver, as if the mass of movements and feelings he has just gone through had taken no time at all. His action has changed nothing, he returns to the same point on a circular time pattern.

Similarly, the student's efforts to escape into the consecutiveness of the far past returns him, through death-related metaphor, to the dangerous present.

IV *Death Witnessed*

In the third chapter, "The Funeral of Patroclus," the ominous-
ness of death increases. From death recounted (Santiago's
through the headlines, the Italian's account) we now proceed
to a witnessing of its results, its ritual. The funeral of Santiago
could just as well be that of the Italian's victim. Thus death,
in the person of the Italian, has penetrated into the Palace,
closer to the student and the American.

The possibility of death occurring within the group is first
suggested by the American, albeit ironically, as he points out to
the Rifle the danger of constantly carrying about his weapon.
The funeral itself remains in the background throughout, a
conclusion to the events of the previous chapter, but also an
anticipation of those to come. The necessary centrality of
the funeral sequence thus becomes patent. The title of the
chapter contains a double meaning. It first refers to the fact
that Santiago was the aide of the present head of government,
his Patroclus. But it also anticipates the disappearance of the
American. Taking the narrator as the central character in the
fiction, though not always its sole object (as Achilles), the
American, for whom the student feels some concern, would
then be his Patroclus. The chapter thus stands as the solution
offered at the level of language to the enigma of the American's disappearance, pointing in fact to his death and confirm-
ing the student's suspicions before the fact.

The accusations of the American become more direct, if never
truly overt, as the chapter progresses. He comes close to situating the responsibility for Santiago's death within the group.
Now the question posed by the newspaper headlines has been
transferred to the streamers held aloft by the procession, as if
come to life. The crowd seems to gather questioningly, threatening, before the Palace, under the men who look on from
the balcony.

As the threat increases, the narrator shifts his perspective to
a conversation at a later moment between himself and the

American, where the latter speaks disdainfully of his own death. The temporal shift continues toward the present of remembrance, fifteen years later, in a pattern parallel to that of chapter 1 (see p. 80 above). With the greater menace of death, the safe isolation of the present is slowly undermined. The grinding of streetcar wheels is described in terms recalling the wheels of the hearse, the vehicle's circuits suggesting thus the perennial historic march of destruction. The city and the narrator have been tainted by the deadly turbulence of the past, "the whole city ... somehow inanimate too: 'Something like bones ...' he thought and he, too, perhaps, like a mere heap of bones on his bench:" (140). Capitalized inscriptions are the present counterpart of those in the past. The caption on the truck of a group of anarchists: "*COLUMNA DE FERRO*"[11] (144), is ironically echoed now by an advertisement on the streetcars, "*FOSFORO FERRERO*" (135). In his wounded present of remembrance, the narrator feels that something in that past escaped him and weighs upon him: "But what was it? What was it? No doubt there was something he hadn't been able to see, something that escaped him, ..." (147–148).

At the end of the chapter the threat around the American grows more precise. As if in preparation for his disappearance, he is described in greater detail. His general semblance is one of grayness; already he seems to belong to death, "as if his whole person, then, with his iron-gray eyes, his silky hair that ... was now no particular color ... that grayish beard on his cheeks, was covered, veiled himself [sic] with a kind of parasitical and colorless growth ..." (153). He has already been absorbed by the prevailing decay: "The whole world was gray, dim, heavy, humid ..." (155).

The beginning of the fourth chapter does not repeat the last sentence of chapter 3.[12] It breaks with the flow of language, apparently initiating a new development with a new sentence. In effect, although the specific events that lead the student to feel that the American has been disposed of by his comrades take place in this chapter, the actual threat to his friend has been spent. In terms of the wider development of the narrative as the growing menace of death to the narrator, it is in this chapter that such a threat first becomes evident; his activities are now tangibly affected, and the guilt that will cause his final anguish is born here. Thus, while the chapter's main concern appears to be the fate of the American, it is in fact the student's own reactions to this fate that remain at the center. The change of roles is clearly implied from the outset. Characteristics of the American's appearance are now the student's: "When you got dressed . . . you merely changed sweat, shifting from the night's sweat to the day's, the only difference being that the latter was white, or rather gray, and clung even closer to your skin" (157). For the first time, the student will focus upon himself, feeling his exhaustion, questioning his motives.

The chapter begins the morning after the night when the American's abduction may have taken place, as the student prepares to meet him at a café. It then returns to the previous evening and night; the last three lines refer once more to the morning. The rendition of this chapter's substance as the remembrance of a remembrance underlines the hypothetical character of the events therein surmised, focuses attention on the only tangible residue, words, and sets the chapter as a counterpart to chapter 2, another memory to the second degree. In this manner, the structure of the novel implies what the events do not make clear: if chapter 4 corresponds to chapter 2, ("The Rifle's Story"), the violence imagined by the student probably did take place; the American was taken to be shot.

The greater involvement of the present of remembrance with the past is established also from the outset; the uncertainty of the recollection which marks the first lines of this section, "but it must have been the next day, since he (the student) had not yet gone out or even shaved" (157–158), introduces plainly the recalling activity in all its doubt. At the same time, we are witnessing a concerted effort on the part of the narrator to mitigate perhaps the events that had just taken place the preceding night, by describing the day as any other day (numerous imperfects of habitual action), and even suggesting some uncertainty about which particular day it happens to be. It is this very concern with seeing the morning as an overly normal one that betrays the narrator's guilt and uncertainty about the night before.

The tokens of death reintroduce specificity and urge the

narration into its developing pattern, although the same effort to weaken their import is once more visible. As the narrator notices the newspaper bought the preceding day, its reading is now automatic, noticeable features reduced to the aspect of the paper itself and the likely repetition of its caption at every vendor's kiosk. Nevertheless, the headline is partially rendered, with emphasis on meaninglessness: "it too, somehow withered, or rather passé, faded, . . . a series of letters selected at random . . . and meaningless . . ." (158). The letters still impose themselves, however, capture thought: they create the transition to the events of the night just passed. The scene specifically recalled at this point is one which, like the first headlines, remains mysterious through what it reveals: a naked woman at a window (the American's, thinks the student), drawing the curtains closed. The description of the curtains suggests the movement of the streamer held aloft during the funeral procession, once more linking that event with this later one. This particular recollection of the previous night's incidents remains still firmly anchored in the morning's thoughts. It represents its first intrusion upon the "present" (recalled present, of course, as opposed to present of remembrance fifteen years later), and the effort to render its events commonplace. In its setting amid the apparent banality of these events much of its mystery is dispersed. The parallelisms of description and the manner in which it is introduced imbue it nevertheless with a portion of the menace contained in the elements (headline, streamer) it recalls.

Inevitably, threatening death-related imagery also gradually penetrates the descriptions that follow. The student's thoughts about the opening hours of the pharmacy in front of him, an obvious further effort to remain in the prosaic, are betrayed by language: "No doubt the shop opened later. Everything began late here, even with the revolution (so that when the American had told him 'tomorrow morning' that might just as well have meant nine o'clock as noon, . . . he would surely find him here as easily as in his room), deciding that most likely it had been looted . . ." (162–163). The last words are equally applicable to the pharmacy and to the American's room. In the next lines, as he contemplates the notice in the store's win-

dow, "*ANALISIS-ORINA—ESPUTOS—SANGRE*"[13] (163), the
student's mind veers definitively to the previous evening's
events. Again the text appears to be controlled by death-related
elements. The argument that precedes the disappearance of
the American is caused precisely by his suggestion to the group
that the druggist's notice would serve effectively as the revolution's slogan. In this elaboration of words, where the creative
activity seems to focus on itself as language, it is fitting that
its mysteries, as well as its revelations, its deaths and struggles,
should all concern the particular interpretation of certain
phrases.

Now in his room the increasing threat posed by thought and
metaphor is assailing the student from all sides. Previous
menaces have become more immediate dangers, gathering
within them the powers of past references, direct suggestions,
and anticipations of the future. The entire city seems a death
trap: "as if it were not simply the night, the darkness that had
replaced the day, but a kind of tide, a warm and opaque lava
that had slowly spread through the streets, the avenues, gradually rising like the water in a lock" (174). It is at this
moment that the narrative initiates a disjunction, similar to
that which in "The Rifle's Story," was characteristic of the
approach of death. The student sees a division growing within
himself: "... he stood up (his body stood up) in hopes (at
least that was the official argument which his body furnished
him and which his mind admitted, although he believed nothing
of the kind) ..." (175). Always, parentheses introduce mobility and fragmentation, the shimmering ripples and eddies that
carve the prose. The menace will enter through the fissures
opened by these incidental statements.

In his effort to ignore his fear, to placate the questioning,
uncertain part of himself, the student tries to turn his attention to other concerns. The acrid smoke from the last cigarillo
of a box given him by the American burns his mouth. The
alternative of reading the newspaper once more nauseates
him, as if his entire body were gorged with a surfeit of its
empty, unanswerable questions. To keep himself occupied, he
tries once more to smoke and finally stamps out the tobacco,
turning to a close examination of the box of cigarillos. The

description of this object appears as a conscious effort on the part of the student to fill his mind and his vision with seemingly innocuous detail. But language betrays this wish and maintains within the description the presence of threat and mystery. As a counterpart to the events of chapter 2, this segment may be generally correlated with the Italian's approach to the restaurant, his actions therein, and his exit onto the street. The first part of the description corresponds to the neon advertisements in front of the establishment: colored arrows, blinking face of a Negro, "ANTILLES RUM" (60). Here we have "arrowtipped and zigzag thunderbolts, ... forked extremities" (180), and the Cuban origin of the cigarillo box, as vision penetrates into the details of the design. Similar correspondences may be established between elements of the box and events inside the restaurant, death and mystery. At its center appears a double riddle, a tarotlike picture "a key floating over the ... waves" (182),[14] and a scene half hidden by a stamp. Numerous details connoting death or violence characterize the depiction: the colors suggest those of generals' uniforms; there is a "lictor's fasces" (182), a "phrygian cap" (182) (revolution); an eagle with its "hooked beak, [ready to tear]"[15] and "powerful spreading talons" (183), near the end of the passage, precedes the capitalized statements of pricing, which are not followed by their corresponding amounts, and restate the suggestion of imperfect knowledge, mystery at the heart of violence.

Other echoes from chapter 2 pursue this parallel development. As he smokes in bed, the student burns his fingers: "so that his hand started, the red glow describing an arc in the darkness, ..." (186). There follow some thoughts about the emptiness of the streets: "nor a car in the street" (186). We recall here the drive through the streets of chapter 2, the sudden turn (arc), and the Italian's gun thrust against his side ("his hand started"). At the same time, this passage announces the noises that awaken him later (the last one being the departure of a car) and their deadly import.

Shortly after, he sees the woman pulling the curtains closed in a window across from his. Some aspects of this apparition also recall a previous one: riding through the city with the

Italian, the sculptured form of a woman suddenly rushed towards them as the car made a sharp turn. But whereas that instant quickly passed, this one (though it lasts a fraction of a second), is expanded through a detailed description and active recall. It is this recall that appeared at the beginning of the chapter. The present one, since it is given within the sequence where it actually took place, in the middle of the night, is in effect the "original" of that previous copy, or memory, restated in the morning; it is a later one chronologically, but an earlier one in terms of the compositional sequence. In a struggle between chronology and structure, the latter is bound to become the controlling factor. The first statement of the vision appears as a parenthesis within a long description of the newspaper (its headline incomplete). This description is first given in as detached a manner as possible, the attention directed at the paper's most superficial characteristics, its lack of mystery. The student's remembrance of the woman's form in this context is but an effort to deny the headline its enigma, empty it of content. It is interjected at a moment when the sense of the words in the newspaper is beginning to form itself,—"but still, when the headline appeared again..." (158) —as an answer to its query; in effect, the student is now convinced that the American was enjoying the woman all the while he was concerned for his safety. Presenting the reason for this thought at this point, he tries to "defuse" the persistent question of the headline "*QUIEN HA MUERTO QUIEN HA ASESINADO QUIEN HA FIRMADO EL CRIMEN*" (178).

The depiction of the cigar box, as we saw, cannot escape the connotative weight of all the preceding narrative, and in particular of chapter 2. Nor can the woman's form (in its second appearance) remain objective or even merely sexually suggestive. In his effort to recall it in all its detail, to extract all its reassuring potential from the vision, the language becomes implausibly specific, invention taking the place of perception, haunting mystery hidden by appearance. The student's belief at the conclusion of the chapter that his concern was misplaced, that the American was making love while he feared for him, seems lame and ineffectual.

V *Death Endured*

Death continues to prevail, progressing from its appearance as headlines or tales from the past (chapters 1 and 2) to
the student's awareness of its results (the funeral in chapter
3), or its nearby occurrence (night noises in chapter 4). At the
same time, we see growing an inner division in the narrator
(through parenthetical clarifications), the first step of the
gradual overtaking of the present by the past. It is in the last
chapter that this duality becomes most patent until the last
lines, where the effort to tear the "residue of himself" from
himself is likened to the parturition of a monster, and produces
a metaphorical death.

The title of the last chapter proposes, ironically, one aspect
of its significance. In effect, the elements which formed the
"Inventory" are found again here, in the "Lost and Found";
their meaning has changed, however, and their new form
precipitates a final and greater loss. This concept of new
meanings, reexamined assumptions, is introduced immediately,
as the student realizes that the poster which in the night had
seemed to him to represent a bombing airplane is in the
light of day that of a youth diving into water. But the pleasant-
ness of this picture is soon dissipated by the surrounding
notices of a more violent nature. The last notice *"NO TOL-
EREIS LOS EMBOSCADOS"*[16] (198) finally reintroduces the
main concern. The student's attitude is now altered, and he
considers that the American is really late: "realizing that it was
ten o'clock, and that even in this country, and even in a period
of revolution, and even taking into account the special circumstances of the girl, ten o'clock must be later than what an
American would call tomorrow morning..." (198); this statement contrasts sharply with that of the previous chapter (see
pp. 162–163).

The next assumption to be discarded will concern the woman.
The student realizes that she was not in the American's room.
The significance of this fact establishes the final division within
himself (begun with the first inklings of uncertainty during
the night), as he tries in vain to open the door to the American's room: "and although he—that is, his body—still stood

motionless in front of the open window, that something in
him which had no need of a body, of limbs in order to move
across the room again, going out..." (201). The newspaper
once more unfolds itself, "as it is said that a corpse can sometimes slowly raise a limb, an arm, or yawn" (202) to show the
haunting, questioning headlines, now applicable to the American more directly, soon to be applicable to himself: "*QUIEN
HA MUERTO*" (202). Henceforth, to a frantic increase in
activity by the student, repeated circuits over the same ground,
aimless wandering, will correspond equally drastic interpene-
trations of past remembered and moment of remembrance. The
efforts by the narrator to remain in the vantage point of his
present are to no avail. His last resort is to insist on the ridiculous character of his actions at that time, repeatedly seeing
himself as "the student, the homunculus, the fledgling, the distant and microscopic double" (236). Now, death has reached
him in his retreat, "the shadow of the Palace itself had reached
him, covering him, making it unnecessary for him to move,
absorbing him, extending over him like a shroud" (235–236).

In a final bid to reject the past by re-creating for it a new
beginning, by starting the narrative, or a parallel one, over
again, he tries to imagine once more, to repeat the process:
"then he would go in, he would climb the three flights...—and
he would go into the office, and among the charred beams...
they would all be there... (247–248). The conditional tense
takes this effort out of the normal context of recall of the
narrative, denying it any generative power; in any case, the
past is now irretrievable ("charred beams"). In the last moments, the narrator surrenders to the evidence of death that has
invaded a present which he merely thought incomplete. He has
brought forth, "like one of those queens in confinement," (251)
in a creation whose underpinning is death itself, a "tiny micro-
cephalic monster,"[17] the dead, decayed revolution: the recollection, instead of justifying his present, leaves it in ruins.

CHAPTER 5

Histoire: *The Mosaic of Memory*

I *Introduction*

*H*istoire (original edition, 1967), published four years after *Le Palace,* remains so far the most massive of Simon's novels. It was awarded the Prix Médicis and immediately hailed by some critics as his best work (Ludovic Janvier, Claude Mauriac, Luc Estang, among others). The reader's initial impression is of an intricate collage of fragmented distant and recent memories, current perceptions, speculation and imagined design. The composition is cemented by mental and metaphorical associations whose arbitrariness is but the mask of a carefully controlled development. Throughout, the visual element predominates, color and contour compensating for the imprecision of remembrance and the precariousness of imagination in passages remote from immediate incident.

Echoes of previous novels run through *Histoire,* characters and situations already encountered, once central incidents now become peripheral to or contained within the all-encompassing endeavor of creative memory. We witness segments of Corinne's childhood, occurrences of the Spanish Civil War, de Reixach's death. The pivotal concerns of preceding works, Eros, death, tradition, retain their importance as centripetal forces which coalesce the fragments of the past.

Recollections of circumscribed periods in time, of specific events, haunting as half-solved riddles and magnets to obsessed memory, erstwhile the sufficient core of a fiction, now appear as individual fragments in the broad sweep of reminiscence. Whereas in earlier novels the forces of history (national or personal) pressed upon the development of particular incidents, their inexorable onrush has now rent the fabric of an entire life, a family, a tradition. The narrator undertakes his reorganization of the past in an effort to contain it, to overcome it perhaps by a final verbalization. It was the same hope that led the narrator of *The Palace* to wager on language and lose, and we can expect a similar conclusion to the present effort. But the interest of the novel is not in the unavoidable end; it is rather in the possibilities of the contention, the shape of the struggle.

Although incident abounds in *Histoire*, the main moments of its development are quickly summarized. The narrator lies in bed, awaiting sleep, watching the branches of the nearest tree. He remembers summer days when he worked late in the night listening to the last sparrows; their cries are reminiscent of the voices of numerous, interchangeable old ladies, last of a disappearing nobility, his mother's and grandmother's visitors. His mother had died wasted by sickness, fiercely attached to a dying past: overzealous, lugubrious catholicism and denial of change. He recalls his childhood and youth with his Uncle Charles and his cousins Paul and Corinne. Forgotten postcards in an old dresser retrace journeys, mainly those of his father, who chose them as his principal means of communication with his mother. He recalls also his participation in the Spanish Civil War and the criticisms it elicited in his conservative home; imagines a possible escapade of Uncle Charles's in Paris, in an artist's milieu, reconstructed from an old photograph; retraces his mother's eventual travels with his father (through postcards also); remembers Lambert, a school fellow, purveyor of the latest fads, class clown.

All these reminiscences occur during the course of one day, as the narrator undertakes to sell some of the furniture of the old house, requests a loan from a bank, and obtains the signature of Paul, now a successful businessman, on a document concerning a small inheritance. At the same time his mind veers toward unexplained incidents pertaining to his honeymoon with Hélène, their breakup, and perhaps her death, or suicide. These thoughts remain unclear, or are not allowed to take definite sequential form in his mind, as if he recoiled from their painful connotations.

The novel is composed of twelve untitled chapters of similar length, except for the seventh (approximately half the usual length), and the last one (slightly longer than the rest). Each chapter contains one central "present" sequence, and allied recollections born of mental and linguistic associations. Although the narrative is told in the first person, the voice is one of investigation and description as much as of analysis. The center of consciousness often functions as pure, depersonalized perception. The point of view becomes at times extremely flexible, imagination allowing it to adopt the coloration of other minds and to animate the stasis of postcards and photographs. At the same time, oscillations between distinct moments of the narrator's own past and that of his family further blur the centrality in the fiction of his present discursive self, in spite of his efforts to assert it.

The subsidence of the teller's role at the expense of language per se has been one of the consistent patterns of Simon's fiction since *The Wind.* In that novel we already noticed language straining at the bonds of a single voice. Long parenthetical statements taxed the continuity of discourse, underlined the insufficiencies of consecutive narration by subverting it. We saw how parentheses introduced the mobility of the incidental, the alternative, parceling the text. Together with the constant use of the present participle they suggest an ongoing effort to fixate movement and to give life to the static; contrary activities which find their temporary solution in the very flow of words.

In *The Palace* the parenthesis extends to its utmost limits whole sections of the narrative appearing in this form. It is in this novel also that we witness the metaphorical destruction of the narrator by his verbalized past, as his reminiscence reaches across a gap of fifteen years to claim him. The prose seems to have acquired a momentum of its own, no longer governable by its fictional originator. In *Histoire* parentheses have diminished; the text now consists of juxtaposed segments of narration, all seemingly incidental to one another, all offering equally important alternatives. The narrator's role as guiding consciousness has been largely dispensed with, and we have as much an arrangement of blocks of language as we do a sequence. The text as such creates its own particular continuity; paragraphs cease without concluding, as a new sequence makes its appearance, and are sometimes continued thereafter. For, although we

have a novel which concerns itself in its entirety with the functioning of recollection, language has now acquired such independence that it develops its own memory as the fiction
progresses; words will recall the constellation of meanings and
suggestions that they acquired in previous pages, in the same
manner as the day's events bring back the past to the mind of
the central character.

The novel bears on each page the weight of its own linguistic
past; it is the creation of a history and also of a memory. The
central consciousness which gives the initial impetus to this
development is constantly submerged by it. Words no longer
describe remembrances as much as they seem to create them,
and the metaphor becomes itself more important than its
source. Because of this inability to exert sufficient control over
the re-creation of his past, the narrator will be unable to escape
the occasional emergence of distressing memories: unhappy
moments with Hélène, his now absent wife. His recollection
will originate and develop along an axis of despair, an increasing awareness of his isolation, the inevitable and unending
aftermath of losing Hélène.

II *The Memory of Language*

From the outset, memory takes precedence over direct perception. We know that Simon has unreservedly opted for the
past as the only adequate recording tense, although "present"
actions and impressions are generally recognizable within its
context. While *Histoire* actually begins in the imperfect, the
unspecific character of this tense allows for sufficient imprecision to deny the text any strong temporal bounds, plunging
the reader into the realm of general reminiscence: "One of
them was almost touching the house and in summer when I
worked late into the night sitting in front of the open window
I could see it or at least its farthest twigs in the lamplight..."[1]
(1). The first clause, through "house," could refer to a "present"
impression, as well as a past one, but its continuation is
definitely set in the past by "when I worked," the text effectively
dispelling the already uncertain immediacy of the event. At the
same time, the refusal to clarify the nature of the object in

question further emphasizes the importance of the text that follows,[2] as repository of all the basic coordinates (temporal and phenomenological) in the sequence.

Additional clues to the functioning of the novel may also be gathered from these lines. The nature of the subject of description is revealed by its periphery (twigs), which in turn is only seen because of the artificial light of the lamp, (the idea of "throwing light on a subject" comes here to mind). The "twigs" belong to the branch, part of a tree which itself remains in darkness. The branches and the tree are mentioned later in terms of sound rather than sight, "a mysterious and delicate murmur spreading invisibly" (1): our vision is limited, and we must infer the rest; in *Histoire* we shall often have to infer the center from the circumference. The movement of the prose has itself traced the very outline of the "twigs" and may also be seen as a correlative of the movement of memory: it spreads its tendrils in all directions, from a darkened source, but more significantly it is also seen as a function of language as much as of perception. Inevitably, the importance of language is then once more patent. To underline it, Simon has begun his novel in "the middle of a sentence," synonymous for him with a beginning "in medias res," since the text here is itself the central event.[3]

The reminiscence proceeds, through verbal associations, to a re-creation of the atmosphere at the narrator's home, this very house where he now is, in his childhood. The branches of the tree introduce the regular visits of ancient, titled birdlike women, (family tree), friends of his mother and grandmother, perennially lamenting the frequent disasters of their kin or the spent glories of superseded times. Once the metaphor—old women = birds—is firmly anchored, it opens the way to a further exploration of their nature not as women but as birds. Their earlier evolutionary stage (reptilian) is then suggested: "certain insectivores, greedy, impassive and precise, snapping up flies and ants..." (5). Similarly avid and intent, the narrator's grandmother would capture the wafer of communion at mass; the service was generally held at the home for his dying mother. Thus, we move from a partial perception ("twigs") to a central memory (sick mother) that will recur later on, pervaded by the general desolation of a decaying past.

The novel will also end in midsentence as the narrator, back in his bed at night, wonders at his fetal presence in his mother's womb, questioning the validity of his enterprise, the reminiscence, as he considers the basic contingency of his own existence. We return to the beginning of the narrative to complete the sentence, language describing the circular limits of its activity, closed upon itself in an ultimate solipsism. The narrator's pursuits during the day have had little effect on his state of mind; if his despair is now more immediate, it is due precisely to the continuing subjection of the present to the past; action has become as much the result as the source of recollection.

This conclusion soon imposes itself as we pursue the idea of circularity. The "present" action of the novel, the undertakings of the narrator during the day, actually begin in chapter 2, as he awakens and rises. This action is preceded by several pages of reminiscence by the narrator in a semiconscious state, which seem to retrace through connotation some of the memories of the previous night (chapter 1).[4] Such echoes of chapter 1 in chapter 2 become more noticeable as the moment of getting up and washing, the first acts of the day, approach. A few compared lines from both will make this clear:

Chapter 1	Chapter 2
"its farthest twigs in the lamplight" (1).	"light spangled through the leaves reflected and projected into the room" (30).
"Grand-mère, she on her prie-Dieu" (5).[5]	"how did it go that prayer" "Du Guesclin dying under his tree" (30).
"two stalks of rambler-roses intertwining, interlacing" (6). "drops of blood scattered" (7).	"and in the next rosette (and between each of them the braid of brilliant flowers and leaves ruby)" (30).
"in thorny Gothic characters notched and interlaced INRI	"and the same cabalistic sign of interlaced letters in each violet

probably or that P and that X in-   lozenge" (30).
terlaced" (7).

"But they weren't the ones I   "the sixth form or the fifth little
could smell so strongly." (6).   freshmen stinking even when
                                 they sang" (30).

Such repetition by analogy links within the same sequence of interior monologue all of chapter 1 and the beginning of chapter 2. It abolishes time, as all repetitions do, and diminishes thereby the importance of "clocked," daytime action. It reintroduces all of the the previous chapter as part of the thoughts preparatory to mental and physical awakening. Only three references are made to the morning's first gestures, reluctantly undertaken under the weight of reminiscence: "and for a moment nothing but that: the cruel and joyous quivering of confetti" (29) as the narrator sees the light filtered through the tree; "then standing, staggering under the weight of the day, thinking" (30); "Moving forward then into the mirror" (31). Even in this last act it is not of himself that the narrator thinks, but of his reflection in the mirror, as if he saw his image advancing towards him from the depths of the past. It should be noted also that we have merely quoted from the one and a half pages of chapter 2 which immediately precede "Moving forward. . . ." The previous pages, 27 to 31, are equally analogous in detail to the principal elements of chapter 1, as we shall see later when considering the first appearance of Hélène. This initial sequence of chapter 2 also maintains, through religious imagery, the presence of the mother's illness and death, while introducing memories.

Further, this connotative iteration underlines the idea of circularity in the context of retraced evening and morning reminiscence, as well as in the broader context of the entire novel: The first actions of the narrator may easily be conceived as the sequel to his last thoughts at the conclusion of the novel. In chapter 2 we see him, "in frayed pajamas, . . . dangling from his navel the limp whitish braided cotton ribbon . . . some visceral link, bleached by the darkness, torn from the livid womb of the night" (31). At the end, as he falls asleep in the night, he imagines himself in his mother's womb: "that bosom

which already perhaps was bearing me in its shadowy taber-
nacle" (341). The darkness of the past is the darkness of the
night and that of the womb. And in the development of the
novel, out of the depth of night in the first chapter rise the
narrator's thoughts of his mother at a point when she is herself
about to enter the final darkness of death.

The ascendancy of reminiscence over action remains as decisive throughout the novel as it was in the first pages of
chapter 2. The narrator's contact with the outside world during
the day is often rendered as mere interruptions of his interior
monologue, occasional intrusions of the immediate into a perennial past. There is no continuity in the actions he undertakes,
very little preparation or aftermath. They often appear as a
function of memory, and since memory is here principally verbalized, that is to say, it is itself a function of language, or its
corollary, action in the novel will also underscore the predominance of the representation as such. Its very sparseness
illustrates the unimportance of the present with regard to the
past. Gesture and movement stagnate, sink into a proliferation
of qualifying comment, fade before the onrush of recollection.

Often given as if it were part of a mental sequence, physical
movement is effectively arrested and almost transformed into
thought. Thus, in chapter 3, the narrator's entrance into the
bank is more a penetration of the mind into the realm of capital
and exchange values than the mere ingress into a building. We
do not see him walking to a chair and sitting; rather his action
appears as the third moment of an intellectual consideration
of his environment and its possible mythical analogues: "thinking of some monster crouching in a corner..." (55), "[per-
ceiving] something like a faint nibbling..." (56),[6] "And
sitting now on an armchair..." (57). Were we to include as
the first element of this series the verb *remembering*, for this
activity continues throughout (though it is seldom explicitly
thus stated), we would have an adequate summary of the
sequence that normally precedes "present" events: "remembering," "thinking," "perceiving," doing. And although action and
perception can also be the basis for further remembrance or
thought, the impact of actuality is so diminished by its mental
concomitants as to be resolved into them. Hence on pages 112

to 116, the narrator considers his present surroundings at a restaurant in terms of a postcard he remembers of a ship's dining room; he does so *after* not only detailing the photograph, but also imagining the dining room transported to a tropical colony, frequented by its typical customers. The transition to the present locale is made by means of an image equally applicable to both situations: "carafes repeated at regular intervals . . . regularly decreasing . . . the images of objects . . . distorted according to the curves . . . the sphere . . ."; ". . . at the bottom the head, a tiny tow-blond blob . . ."; "Looking up then, discovering her . . ." (113–114).

The paragraphs preceding the quoted lines give a striking concentrated vision, historical and geographic, of colonialism from the point of view of food, sharply underlining the incongruity of white men's habits transposed to a jungle setting: all this emerges from the postcard. The vision moves from immobility to movement to immobility (postcard–liner–land), and from a representation (postcard) to imagined activity (transportation to colonial setting) to another representation (reflection on carafe). This passage, from the broad sweep of recall (the postcard itself is remembered) to the deceiving narrowness of actual sight, clearly underscores the paucity of mere sensation. At the same time, it sets the presence of the narrator in the restaurant as a meager counterpart to creative memory. In contrast to the "Sauternes and shell-fish," and the announcement "Live lobsters today" (113) at the imagined restaurant, the present menu bears incomprehensible signs: "Then staring without managing to decipher the meaning, the lines" (114). Soon the text will once more veer towards the richer depths of memory and metaphor. The goods of the earth are seen transformed into banknotes and back into food, again the passage from a vast vision to a commonplace event.

III *Love*

The subservience of the present to the past becomes all the more evident when we consider the relationship of the day's main activities to their inferable cause. The narrator applies for a loan, sells some furniture, obtains a signature on a deed. In each case, albeit such sentiments are never actually expressed, he anticipates unwanted pity, concern, or curiosity from the people he talks to with regard to Hélène. The old man whom he encounters before entering the bank is content to pursue his ineffectual existence as long as he can remember his youth. The dealer in antiques thrives on the disasters of others, and Paul, with his friends, speculates on future values. Each character represents both a success and a failure from the point of view of the narrator: he sees the old man as a failed nonentity who has achieved a *modus vivendi* that will sustain him until his death. The dealer's business is clearly viewed as scavenging, but her increased prosperity is undeniable. Paul's real estate deals are often questionable, yet he is rich and stays ahead of the game. The narrator has failed in the two areas which are most commonly seen as measures of accomplishment: the economical and emotional planes. While he refuses the types of accommodations to the world that he sees exemplified by the people he encounters, he remains unable to supersede old failures. Though he rejects the present, he seems condemned to relive a past that is disintegrating under the impact of the most recent of his losses, that of Hélène. Indeed, the memories of his former wife, which he generally tries to suppress, play a major role in the development of the fiction, constituting the principal threat to the narrator's control over his reminiscence.

Except for chapters 4, 11, and 12, references to Hélène are infrequent and generally indirect, but in actuality her presence (or rather her absence) pervades the entire narration: every departure is her departure; every loss, her loss. She first intrudes into the narrator's thoughts early in chapter 2, at a time when he is particularly vulnerable, bearing the weight of the night's recollections. Not fully awake, his control over memory is as yet imperfect.

We saw above how the thoughts of the previous night are reintroduced, through an analogous recollection, in the moments preceding the narrator's first morning activities. It is amid these thoughts that Hélène is recalled, underscoring from the outset at least a strong kinship between the two sets of memories. The initial progression of this second chapter is parallel to that of the first in that we begin with a peripheral perception and plunge therefrom into the realm of reminiscent metaphor. In this case, the sequence starts with the cries of birds, suggesting the grinding of an old cart and the labored setting out of a protesting, tired old world. As the narrator opens his eyes, he sees one bird against the grayness of dawn and compares its emerging outline to that of the earth from night. The next thoughts unite cries and color into a mythological metaphor recalling the black Stymphalian birds, and moves from it to the old women introduced in the last chapter: "the eyes like the *cabochons* of long hatpins thrust into their toques . . . like the eyes of those flies that feed on corpses shrieking tearing me making their meal of disasters of griefs staring at me with their empty woebegone birds' eyes in which petrified, suspended, tranquil . . ." (27). The process is one of convergence, an increasing number of powerfully connotative elements bearing down upon the defenseless mind. The narrator's effort to avoid the painful associations becomes an unsuccessful attempt to move: ". . . and I trying to move to turn back, then submerged . . . (27).

The memory of Hélène which now overwhelms him is that of her final departure. In its detail the pattern of this emergence in the narrator's consciousness is akin to a pulsation. A single initial perception is soon multiplied; there follows a gradual focalization toward one final, uniquely suggestive image, gathering the emotional impact of all that precedes it. The remembrance proceeds from the narrator's initial effort to resist, in which he sees only himself ("and I trying to move") to an accumulation of remembered sense impressions: "she and I, and the locomotive panting"; "the hissing of the two steam jets"; "her wide enormous eyes staring at me but no tears only lakes"; "the little train of baggage carts"; "the hand suddenly jumped the space of two minutes" (27-28). There follows a gradual contraction of the perceived world: "she and I still standing in front of each other the machine holding and releasing its steam"; "as if at moments all sound disappeared and nothing but the two of us standing in that silence, as if the whole world were dead, swallowed up, as if nothing else existed, except her face . . ." (28). The final reduction is an actual erasure of everything except the eyes: "and not even the greenish side of the car behind her, not even the collar of her coat, her hair, her forehead, her mouth: only her eyes—" (28).

Although she appears in the fiction only sporadically when verbal associations become too powerful for the narrator to suppress her memory, Hélène remains the focal point of the novel's development; her image echoes and anticipates all the other reminiscences that constitute the narration. In this her first appearance, for instance, she is linked: (1) with the idea of departure and absence as expressed already in the first chapter, that is to say, mainly the absence of Henri (the narrator's father) from his wife (the locomotive is "*au bout du quai*"—"at the end of the platform"—(27–28); *quai* applies in French both to seaports and train stations, and Henri seems forever to be on an ocean voyage); (2) with the narrator's suffering, in its turn reminiscent of his mother's agony; (3) with the imagery of water, of eyes as "lakes of tears" (28) which is also suggestive of the departure motif and the ocean; (4) generally, with images of birds and therefore aspects of the old women seen in the first chapter.

The narrator sees his loss of Hélène as the result of a tradition exemplified by the old women he remembers as a child visiting his mother and grandmother. It is precisely as he tries to escape from the company of another representative of this tradition in the person of an elderly man that he explains to him: "Yes it's a family tradition of ours widowhood I mean . . . Yes Transmissible to the men of the clan by uterine means . . ." (54). The statement is applicable to himself, insofar as he identifies with his mother more than his father, as well as with his Uncle Charles, a widower also. His own "widowhood" will therefore appear to him as the repetition of an ancestral pattern; when he considers the circumstances of his mother's conjugal life, a prolonged solitude, he will be reiterating the one fundamental fact of his own failed marriage. Similarly, the recollections of his Uncle Charles's visit to his wife's grave will be an expression of his personal despair, and the detailed description of a possibly compromising photograph of Charles's youth will stand for the unavowed confession of his own mistake. In this manner again, Hélène stands at the hub of the fiction's circuit. The reminiscence, as we shall further see, is a result of her departure, and the narrator sees her departure as the result of what he remembers, the principal elements of his own life. What we have then is not a fiction composed of narrative segments connected by free association, but rather a selective, biased vision of the past. Biased insofar as it reflects the general mood of despair resulting from the narrator's failed marriage. Selective in that he tries to suppress, as much as he can, specific segments of his past concerning that very failure. Under these conditions there is little room for free association. The presence of Hélène will find its expression in all the other less distressing reminiscences that are analogous to what her loss represents, and which the narrator prefers to recall. Her memory will break through into the fiction generally as a result of unusually suggestive sequences, pervaded with strongly allusive "generative" words or imagery: eyes, water, erotic scenes (remembered or read), trains, boats, death, travel, birds, and so on.

The narrator, as he tries to free himself from his past through organized reminiscence, cannot prevent words from gradually acquiring ever greater implicative power. At the end of the novel, the text will be so suffused with connotations leading directly to Hélène that he will no longer be able to avoid the most painful episodes he had tried to suppress. From another point of view, however, his memories constantly deal with Hélène, since she is at the origin of the total recollection and remains throughout as its center of reference. Nevertheless, she represents a disruptive force threatening the narrator, one that can only be deflected or tentatively regulated but not contained. Significantly, the words introducing her initial capture of the narrator's mind ["then submerged again foundering" (27)], recall directly those of the novel's epigraph by Rilke ("It submerges us. We organize it. It falls to pieces. We organize it again and fall to pieces ourselves"), clearly implying the chaotic effect of her presence upon the whole enterprise.

IV *Death and Tradition*

Linked also to Hélène and to her multiple echoes throughout the narration emerge other central motifs of Simon's fiction:

death, love's counterpart, and tradition. As the object of the
narrator's love, she is also the source of the obverse, darker
side of passion, the death wish, which in Simon accompanies
almost all erotic circumstance. In this instance, memories of
Hélène are almost invariably joined by death-related imagery or
reminiscences directly linked with death. These thoughts apply
both to Hélène herself and to the narrator.

Hélène's first appearance follows a number of death images
which point to the intensity of the narrator's suffering (see
pp. 28 to 31). Ubiquitous death affects generally both the
narrator and Hélène herself, whose departure was followed
by her suicide, the main reason perhaps why acquaintances
circumspectly avoid any mention of her to the narrator; he,
however, invariably anticipates just such inquiries: "wondering
if being half-dead gave him the right to ask about Hélène
openly" (39); "restraining...her questions about Hélène"
(192). Although there is no explicit statement about Hélène's
suicide, a number of details definitely point to it, creating an
accumulation of allusion that allows for no other interpretation.
Memories of her assault the mind of the narrator in chapter
4, a crucial segment of the fiction bristling with representations
of and references to death. Indeed, most of the deaths which
are mentioned at one point or another in the novel appear in
this chapter, either directly mentioned or indirectly referred to.

It is in this chapter also that the most specific reminiscences
of Hélène emerge. The narrator recalls his conversation with
Corinne when he told her of his impending marriage. He
remembers Hélène's vision of Greece as "a huge ancient skeleton
half-lying in the sea" (83). Further memories of their trip
through Greece strengthen Hélène's ties with water and death.
Some of the happiest moments of their honeymoon were spent
after Hélène would come into the narrator's bed wet from the
ocean in the early morning. Allusions to tombs abound in their
visits to ruins and museums; even the Greek inscriptions they
examine suggest the alliance of sex and decay: "...at close
range their incision, the edges crushed or splintered was no
more than a vague furrow..." (96)[7]. The reference of these
lines to Hélène's own pudenda is made clear later in this
chapter, as the narrator recalls the day when she had shaved

her genitals: "... it was like those of little girls plump infantile tender..." (101). Hellas, a country of rivers (specifically mentioned as such by her) surrounded by the ocean is directly suggestive of Hélène in her element, water, and contains intimations of death. As he now remembers, the narrator could perceive within her even then the growing menace: "her back like an enigmatic wall enclosing hiding that kind of tragic melancholy that black somber thing that was already inside her like a core of death" (89). A further inference arises from the newspaper headlines concerning another woman's recent death, first mentioned in this chapter: "SHE THROWS HERSELF OUT OF THE FOURTH FLOOR WINDOW..." (93–94), a statement turning the general allusions to death into a more particular reference to suicide. Intimately related not only to his loss of Hélène but also to his passion, incessant guilt feelings constantly intrude into the narrator's remembrance and further shackle his effort at organization. The first open expression of such concerns follows shortly after Hélène's initial appearance in chapter 2: "The enchanted cup emptying even as it is filled. Or rather cupula. Culpa mia.... eyes closed, still splashing over my lowered face two or three useless handfuls of water..." (p. 32). The sequence, cup–cupula–culpa, joins eroticism (cupula–vulva) with guilt, and the occasion (washing his face) introduces, through water, thoughts of Hélène. A transition is created by means of the water to his mother, her death, and religion: "the so to speak aquatic décor which the mirror doubles and in the center of which stands my own double still swaying as he emerges from the maternal darkness,... blinking Father let this cup pass from..." (32–33). Hélène and the narrator's mother are thus linked by the text in guilt and death.

Together with his mother and Hélène, Corinne plays a central role in the narrator's memories. As opposed to his mother in her later years,[8] Corinne is also closely associated with water, that is, with sex. The first mention of her already establishes this relationship, although very faintly, since she is as yet a child: " 'She is very happy and at this moment is playing outside in the garden with the Rivière[9] children...' " (13). In chapter 4, one of the personal memories that the

narrator has of Corinne places her in close proximity with
water, now in a more definite manner: "so pretty . . . the edge
of her summer dress gaping their tips pale pink like a swelling
the bouquet of ivy with its corpse-smell peppery earthen . . .
her hand no longer stirring the water" (74). At the same time
the reference to "corpse-smell peppery" reminds us of the early
pages and the pervasive odor at his mother's bedside, maintaining still a link between guilt (his desire for Corinne) and
death.

Passion, death, and guilt remain throughout indissolubly
linked as part of the tradition, personal and ancestral, that
burdens the narrator's existence. As a youth, his awareness
of sex was doubly tainted with guilt: the attraction he felt
for his cousin was compounded by his realization of her
promiscuity; his own erotic dreams were suffused with visions
extracted from a forbidden book of his uncle's library, Apuleius's
Golden Ass. In both cases, sex seemed an unattainable, arduous
experience (the difficult Latin had to be translated!).

Thwarted passion, erotic failure are part of the tradition that
crushes the narrator. In his relationship to this tradition he
follows, in spite of himself, in the steps of his Uncle Charles
and his mother, while standing opposed to those who forsake
or attack it: Corinne, Paul, and Lambert, his friend. Corinne
seems the personification of sex and rebelliousness. She is un-
daunted by formalities and scorns appearances. Nevertheless,
she marries a de Reixach, deceives him constantly, and inherits
his wealth when he conveniently dies in Flanders. Paul is
interested in immediate, material success; he has an instinctive
ability to be in the right place at the right time in rugby, his
favorite sport, an ability he manages to transfer to the world
of business. Lambert's scorn for tradition is born mostly of
envy, but his shrewdness, vulgarity, and gall equip him
thoroughly for his avocation: regional politics.

The narrator's own rebellion against traditional impositions
takes two forms: on the one hand, by marrying Hélène, he
wants to overcome the hold that the memory of his mother
and his latent feelings for Corinne still have on him, but he
fails. On the other, he wants to reject the reactionary politics
and conservative catholicism of the family by fighting in Spain

on the Republican side, another venture failed. These two failures are directly reflected by his activities during the day: they are the result of a conjugal and a material disaster, both of which are implied by his sale of some family furniture from the ancestral home where he lived with Hélène. The effort to review his past, to organize it, is also an attempt to deny its power over him, an enterprise akin to his interpretation of Lambert's irreligious puns: "Arsenal of puns and spoonerisms supposed to free him by the magic of the Word from maternal superstitions and the lessons of the Catechism." (31). Containing it in words and reliving it, he tries to extract himself from his previous life, from temporality. But the magic of language holds unsuspected powers that make of this ultimate reaching for freedom a final admission of subjection.

V *Representations*

1. *Pictures.* The novel comprises two principal kinds of perception. The narrator's awareness of the "active" present—his surroundings and his affairs during the focal day—gathers around them sequences of personal recollection or imagined incident. His examination of the "static" present—the postcards he discovers in an old dresser and their stamps, a photograph of his Uncle Charles, a box of cigars, a chocolate bar, bank notes—likewise elicits verbal reminiscences.

By enveloping his present in a cocoon of remembrance and imagination, the narrator hopes to immobilize it, transform it into the latest moment of a long process, and thereby separate his inner self from it. The present is cruel because it is indifferent while demanding attention; its very mobility is painful. Awakening consciousness recoils from the sharp glimmer of early sunlight, "the cruel and joyous quivering of confetti" (see p. 29). The narrator will tend to fixate the unpredictability of the present by framing it in a visual composition, an imaginary design or a memory sequence. In his early moments of wakefulness this attempt consists of a simple stabilization in terms of perspective: "the converging lines of their parallel rows drawn by the perspective toward an imaginary point beyond the wall opposite" (28). As he proceeds into the day and his mind achieves firmer control, he allows imagination to absorb his surroundings and situate them in the more rigid cadre of past reference. Linked directly to personal memories of the past, they become largely a part of his general recollection.

While the present needs to be circumscribed, contained by the past, the past itself (in particular those portions of it whose residue consists of old postcards, letters, and one photograph, and in which the narrator played no role) must be reinvented, brought to life again. At other times, the animation is not transmitted to the object of description, but merely suggested by the very mobility of the descriptive sequence itself, that is to say, by the unusual movement of the language, with frequent incidental statements, numerous qualifying phrases, many verbs.

The most important sequence of this type, where a picture is transformed into a detailed incident with its antecedents and aftermath, concerns an old photograph of Uncle Charles, whose examination extends over one entire chapter (9) and large segments of the following one. It shows his uncle in a painter's atelier, seated beside a half-clad model; we also see, standing in front of the easel, another couple and a thin woman, perhaps the artist's wife. The narrator is fascinated by the photograph, out of place amid the profusion of old postcards. It reveals a hidden aspect of his uncle, whose frequent trips to Paris intrigued him even as a child. The banal and yet mysterious situation draws the mind into it as into a vortex. Vaguely recalled references to Uncle Charles's infidelity seem to find in it an explanation, and yet nothing can be definitely inferred. The scene itself, a picture of an artist painting a scene with a window open to other open windows across the lane, creates the suggestion of a multiplicity of "frames," of representations one within the other.

The idea of *"construction en abyme"* arises from the analogy between the narrator's situation and that of the reader. The narrator feels that the photograph is an indication of something about his uncle, but he does not know what that may be, and he must admit that the mystery could be a construct of his mind. Nevertheless, his description seems to be more an effort to decipher an enigma than a mere transcription of photographic detail. The very fact that it is a photograph, rather than the usual, impersonal postcard, already solicits unusual attention. The reader, on the other hand, also seeks the solution to the enigma, generally skirted by the reminiscences in the novel, at whose core there likewise seems to be a development both commonplace and intriguing. Although we know that the narrator deceived his wife, through his own admission, we have little information about this circumstance. Could it be with Corinne, whose memory can still arouse him? In like manner, we may infer Hélène's suicide, but no specific statement is made about it.

The parallelism in the two situations arises then, first, from a similarity in conjugal circumstances between Uncle Charles and the narrator. But more importantly it is from the analogous situations of the narrator and the reader, both attempting to decipher a possible enigma within an endlessly receding set of representations, that there emerges a coincidence of concern. In the following chapter (10) the narrator substitutes himself for his uncle, a last attempt to penetrate beyond the glossy surface of the photograph. His attention focuses at this time primarily on the painter's model, the center of the secret itself; dressed in a man's jacket, her partial nakedness is an image of her double, semimysterious nature. The secret is indeed revealed in the last words she says to the narrator-as-Charles:

"That must be fun; I'd like to
What?
She stuck out her chin toward the roughed-in picture
I don't know All those colors" (254).

We cannot but smile at this liquidation of the riddle. The first words seem to hold some vague erotic promise, but the narrator's attention is directed by the woman away from herself and to the painting: all is contained in the representation per se. In this manner the *construction en abyme* reaches its climactic conclusion by directing the reader also to the narration itself as the self-reflecting plot of the novel. As the attention of the narrator is shifted from this scene, the individuals in it lose the concreteness that his identification with Uncle Charles had provided, to become even less than what they were on the photograph: "while the outlines of the figures are increasingly blurred, erased, no longer leaving anything but immaterial, increasingly diaphanous streaks like dubious vestiges" (255).

As a mirror image of the novel's design, this segment effectively reveals at least the general direction of its development, while functioning both as its possible generator and its condensed summation. By introducing a fixed image within the composition and then allowing the fiction in its turn to penetrate it (e.g., the narrator substituting himself for his uncle) a double representational movement is established, whereby portrayed fixity is freed and action is itself fixated. The reader's attention is constantly redirected to the fictional character of the narrative, his mind sustained at a level of awareness that understands the relation exclusively as what it is, a self-enclosed universe whose justification and reference is language alone.

2. *Texts.* Corresponding to chapter 9 in the twelve-chapter scheme of the novel, chapter 4 contains a concentration of written counterparts to the main fictional motifs that create a similar play-within-a-play situation, intended to point out the analogies inherent in apparently unrelated matter. Whereas the effect of chapter 9 was to enlighten us, by way of the "absent" mystery, as to the paramount role of the narration per se as opposed to its possible source (loss of Hélène and subsequent guilt of the narrator), chapter 4 points in the other direction, underlining the substratum common to all its seemingly disparate elements. Both sequences lead directly to language.

As we have stated, it is in this chapter that the narrator informs Corinne of his coming marriage to Hélène (see p. 108 above). Here also is given an early argument with his bride, which he sees as the beginning of their rift. The chapter opens with his transaction at the bank, whose marbled vastness recalls ancient ruins, and ends with Uncle Charles's letter about his wife's grave, and a description of some postcards from Henri. Upon leaving the bank, the narrator thinks of the history of capital and in particular the significance of battles (Waterloo in this case) in stock market transactions. The thought of battles introduces de Reixach's death and Corinne. The heat of the sun after the coolness of the bank reminds him of Greece and Hélène, though as yet he remembers her in their earlier, unclouded days.

The narrator's marriage to Hélène and his adventure in war-torn Spain, as we pointed out, are both expressions of his desire to rebel against the impositions of his early life. They both find their "literary" correlative in apparently extraneous excerpts from other books: a text of the "Book of Pharsalus" from Caesar's *Civil Wars* parallels the Spanish memories; erotic passages from *The Golden Ass* correspond to the honeymoon. Other accounts, on the Russian Revolution, restate the idea of civil rebellion, while Charles's letter describing his wife's grave pursues the analogy with the protagonist's own marital collapse.

The narrator's encounter with "capital" in the bank recalls the first total revolution against it in Russia. His own romantic effort to combat it was unsuccessful (the Spanish Civil War was lost by the left). He was unable to forget Corinne in Hélène's arms, a condition reflected by Apuleius's text and uniting them both: "haec simul dicens insenso grabatulo scaling the bed she aCCosts wing of her loosened hair flying figure (the twin loops of the *l*) softened slanted by running the two C's like two backs or rather the same back..." (102).[10] Corinne (C) and Hélène (*l*) are inseparable in his mind. He loses one because of the other. Once more, love and death also are inseparable, Apuleius joins Caesar. Tradition remains, though transformed perhaps: The Spanish Civil War fails, and so does the Russian Revolution in terms of its avowed initial goals. All lost women are one, and they are all linked by the same sounds and the same imagery (water, birds); all wars are one, the postcards of battlefields all show the same picture; money levels all men in their greed. Presenting together apparently disconnected elements from different times and of different intent, the text creates its own analogies and generates verbal anticipations and echoes that unite this fragmentation into an indivisible whole.

This unifying substructure is visible both at the times when the narrator seems to have his attempted organization of the past well in hand and at the times when he is unable to prevent the connotative burden of language from calling forth dreaded recollections, destroying his pattern. In chapter 8, for instance, while he still maintains reasonable control over his memory, inevitable echoes and analogies emerge that link the dealer in antiques with other women in his past. When she is first seen, she is related to them mainly through direct associations, first to Corinne, then to his mother, later to Hélène. But her predatory gaze upon all available objects situates her among the more likely company of old women who were also present at the earlier family disasters. All the associations of the first chapters are elicited; in particular, his mother's illness. This and religion are in their turn tied to his experiences in the Spanish Civil War; he remembers his mother's ceaseless pilgrimages, in search of a cure, to miraculous sites where multitudes of cripples are "carted in a clatter of crutches . . . litanies hymns . . . and imprecations spattered pellmell from toothless mouths with the sticky fragments of . . . food rice crusts of bread wafers or sandwiches" (190). "Crutches," "toothless mouths," "sandwiches" recall a particular episode of the war in Barcelona where a hunchback "brought out an already half-eaten sandwich which he began gnawing" (162).

Thus, words allow the text to contrast and unite segments of memory otherwise unrelated and to create linguistic undercurrents that will gradually sap the narrator's arduously erected structure of reminiscence. In the last segment, visions of Hélène inexorably emerge from almost all the recollections where the narrator's mind seeks refuge, in a superficially chaotic proliferation of the elements of the preceding eleven chapters.

VI *The Wheel of Remembrance*

The basic structure of the novel arises then from the narrator's effort to organize his remembrance in order to minimize and absorb his painful marital experience, leaving the consequences of his separation from his wife (her probable suicide and his responsibility) an unwritten blank. In order to allay his guilt he

needs to contain his past, to structure it. As in *The Palace,* this
enterprise fails because of the associative momentum acquired
by language, and instead of separating himself from his memories, he is submerged by them. The epigraph of the book indicated as much and gave us the clue to this underlying structure.

The first part of Rilke's statement "It submerges us. We
organize it. It falls to pieces" describes the development of
chapters 2, 3, and 4. The actual daily activities of the narrator
begin in the morning, with chapter 2. We already noted (p. 107,
above) the parallelism that exists between the beginning of this
chapter and the first sentence of the epigraph. Its continuation
consists of a systematic reordering of the reminiscences of chapter 1 and the introduction of memories that will be later reexamined, particularly those dealing with his parents and his uncle.
Chapter 3 reflects a greater attention to detail in recollection and
would correspond then to Rilke's "we organize it." It is the only
chapter where the effort to remember—"But exactly" (61)—is
repeated three times, and where the exact nature of this attempt
is also stated: "Thinking: not dissolve, fall to pieces" (71). The
reference to the epigraph could not be clearer, or the realization
by the narrator of imminent danger to himself (also in the epigraph), in the event of failure. "It falls to pieces" reflects the
apparent chaos of chapter 4, where extraneous texts, old and
recent, appear side by side with memories, and fragments of
the present. Hélène also dominates here, drawn by the unusual
concentration of unchecked recollections and the magnetlike
force of the newspaper headline ("She throws herself . . ."),
whose dangerous associations create in the narrator moments of
uncertainty. It is for him in any case safer, if Hélène's memories
are unavoidable, to remember their early days; he recalls in
particular their honeymoon in Greece.

Chapters 5 to 10 would correspond to "We organize it again,"
and in effect they contain the moments of the novel where the
narrator seems best to control his remembrance. Hélène emerges
not once; the conscious effort to arrange his material is again
apparent at the end of chapter 8, where certain times of the
day are assigned to a series of postcards, a vain attempt to situate them in time as they are in space. Chapter 9 is wholly given
to the study of Uncle Charles's photograph and remains through-

out a fixed description. It is given mobility in chapter 10 as the narrator attempts to incorporate the scene into his own past. Towards the end of the chapter 10, circumstance begins to accumulate dangerous associations. His drive to Paul's home takes him to the seashore and the proximity of water (water = Hélène). There he finds a Greek, friend and partner of his cousin. Paul has given his wife a diamond: "It's our anniversary she said The smell of the sea on them shellfish Conches" (257). (Precious stones, like frozen water, are also reminiscent of women. The old women's eyes were like *cabochons*, that is to say, dark stones. "Shellfish Conches" suggests cup, vulva, and water, and also Hélène.) Furthermore, Paul's little daughter is called Corinne; she is wet, in a bathing suit, and unfriendly. Paul's wife asks him to stay for dinner: "In her eyes and on her face a kind of perplexity of pitying curiosity and also a vague repugnance..." (262). The narrator guesses the unasked question about Hélène on her lips.

All this prepares us for the final breakdown (11, 12, 1), "We organize it again and fall to pieces ourselves." This time the defeat undoes the narrator totally, to the point where he questions the significance and purpose of his entire life; he asks the last question preparatory perhaps to trying again a final reconstruction of himself and his past: "a kind of gelatinous tadpole coiled around itself with its two enormous eyes its silkworm head its toothless mouth its cartilaginous insect's forehead, me?" (341). As in *The Palace*, moments of great stress and danger bring with them the desire to start anew, characterized by the occasional use of the conditional tense. The presence of a reincarnation of Corinne in chapter 10 suggests the idea of circularity and the true closing of the novel, not with the narrator a grown man in his bed, but with him as a child, in the same bed, watching the light on the tree branches, remembering until morning his dying mother and her absent husband. (chapter 1).

Upon examining this general pattern we perceive that the periods of greater control by the narrator are marked by longer segments devoted to each remembrance; as his effort breaks down, these segments become shorter and interpenetrate one another, thereby allowing the relationships between words and their connotations to become more visible, in contrast to those between mnemonic associations. Likewise, there is a gradual, albeit by no means rigid, transition towards more recent memories, including those pertaining to his activities in the recent "present." A return to thoughts of his adolescence takes place near the end of the novel, as a prelude to another beginning (Corinne taking drugs), and the last lines, as we saw, go back to his imagined prenatal existence.

With *Histoire* Simon approaches a new stage in his prose, in which the traditional elements of plot tend towards dispersion. As the title indicates, *Histoire* is both the decadence of a tradition, and a single story; but as in the general history we know, all that we have left is a "telling." The facts disappear beneath their rendering in language, and the discontinuities of the past are filled not by events but by words. To underline the opposition between events and the language that contains them, Simon breaks the consecutiveness of both incident and syntax, allowing another type of sequence to emerge, that of analogy. In this manner, he liberates language from its ties to the habitual relationships of reality, uncovering its less visible ones, those that may bridge the impossible distance between two events with the available proximity of two words.

CHAPTER 6

The Battle of Pharsalus:
Confluent Languages

I *Introduction*

INCREASINGLY, Simon's fiction requires careful rereading. The true matter of the novel now resides at a level which we customarily bypass, the self-referential capacity of language, in contrast to the preconceived external reality that traditional fiction relates to and that we move in, often heedless of the words, our means of access.

There is an even greater dispersion of surface plot material in *The Battle of Pharsalus* than there was in *Histoire*. For instance, we no longer follow a focal recollection, and the role of memory has greatly diminished. There remains, of course, the unavoidable recording consciousness, but patent confusions about its identity are eventually introduced, directing our attention to the surface activity of language rather than to its presupposed source. On the other hand, recognizable material from that previous novel allows the reader the impression of navigating over slightly familiar waters: we meet Uncle Charles once more, and also, very quickly, Corinne and Paul. Under one of his guises, the observer seems to hold the same relationship with the family as in *Histoire*. Uncle Charles's ties with the artist Van Velden and his model, derived from a photograph in *Histoire*, are here further explored in their own right. The Battle of Pharsalus itself (as the title shows) has now moved from an ancillary to a central position in the narrative.

To the receding significance of recollection corresponds an increase in the importance of purely linguistic means of invention. The role of free association was already in *Histoire* less crucial than it appeared, its function largely taken over by the self-echoing virtue of words. Now the fiction-generating role has been assumed by language alone. Puns, analogies, connotations, spoonerisms, all come into play to create a complex self-originating literary structure. All levels of action, imagination, and description are bridged and subsumed by writing; action is arrested, imagination becomes realized, description breathes life into objects. Sculptures, graffiti, paintings, movies, ancient texts, all are transformed into verbal activity. Traversing all representations, language contains them all in fact and in potential. The world of the novel spans time and space, action becomes history and ancient battles are fought in our day. The all-encompassing possibilities of words propose, in a narration whose action is its own development, a plot far richer than the mere gestures of men limited by circumstance. In this sense, any decantation of incident from its linguistic matrix must remain temporary, a tactic valid only in that it allows the establishment of recurring signposts in the narrative.

As he sits at a sidewalk café, watching a window on the fifth floor of a building across the street, a man sees a pigeon flying across the sun, black on yellow. Looking down he notices several youths at another café across from him, and some people emerging from a subway exit. He remembers his Uncle Charles, now dead, and the Latin translations he struggled through in his presence, in particular, a segment of Caesar's *Civil War* on the Battle of Pharsalus. Uncle Charles lectures him on the importance of language and the need for a modicum of education in a supposedly civilized society. Thoughts of sign language, of "argot," suggest to him through word associations the room behind the window, where he imagines his mistress making love with a red-haired man. The entire sequence will undergo several elaborations, and one partial verbatim repetition. In each instance the lovers stop as O (the observer) furiously bangs on the door.[1] The lovemaking itself is frequently displaced by thoughts on the Battle of Pharsalus and O's trip to Pharsala with a friend, in search of the battlefield. Intermingled with these principal reappearing sequences, O recalls some desperate moments when his life was in danger during World War II, and comments on some painted scenes, mostly of battles.

The first part of the novel concerns itself principally with

these elements as immediate, imagined, or remembered incidents. In the second part there is a reexamination of the Battle
of Pharsalus, some memories of the narrator's childhood with
his mother and grandmother at Lourdes, a conversation with
the wife of an artist friend (Van Velden, whose model is probably O's, now Charles's, mistress). Other segments introduced
here are: an incident from O's barracks memories where he and
his companions are wary witnesses to the ravings of a red-haired
drunken soldier; the careful description of a broken-down Mc-
Cormick agricultural machine previously encountered as part of
the landscape at Pharsala; a train journey from Paris to the
Balkans and back; the diagrammatic rendition of O's field of
perception as he sits at his café table. The third and last part
undertakes a restatement of most of the previous material seen
principally from the vantage point of the train voyage through
Europe. The narrative concludes on the image of the pigeon
crossing O's field of vision and his writing down on a sheet of
white paper his initial impression of this flight as black on
yellow.

The opening section of the novel is entitled "Achilles running
motionless" and bears as its epigraph the twenty-first stanza of
Valéry's *Graveyard by the Sea* (*Cimetière Marin*). Without
engaging in an elaborate analysis of these lines, it would be fair
to say that the metaphors therein suggest arrested movement,
and therefore arrested duration: "And the sun . . . A tortoise
shadow."[2] Any semblance of a temporal framework such as that
in *Histoire*, which allowed us to relate the protagonist's thoughts
to several important moments of a twenty-four hour cycle, has
now been entirely discarded.

The main continuity of the fiction being verbal, normal chronology is of little consequence. For the first time, the beginning
of the novel is given in the present, and establishes this tense
as the point of departure of all other sequences. The time we
deal with is the "time of syntax," the present of writing. The
successiveness of events is linked not to their situation along a
temporal vector, but to their pertinence in the flow of narration.
Hence, it is not a successiveness of events, but one of fragments
of narrative. The abolition of customary duration arises from
Simon's insistence on restricting the activity of fiction to its

proper field and intensifying the reader's awareness of these limits. It is consequent with the decision to burn the bridges that allow the reader to install his vision of reality within the confines of a narrative; that is to say, it questions the habits of thinking that look in the fictional universe for a replica of our own. To this end, description and recall, accustomed instruments of realism, become antirealistic through overemphasis and direct our attention to the act of describing.

In *The Battle of Pharsalus* the operation of time as well as that of reality will be revealed in the threefold contrast between reality as we expect it, reality as a representation, and the representation as its own reality. Reality as we expect it would appear to allow for the passing of time, if only in short periods. There are two main sequences of events, hence two possible temporal progressions, in the first part of the novel: the incidents taking place before the observer at his café table, and the search for the battlefield near Pharsala. At this initial level, the attack on duration will be directed by suggesting not its inexistence, but its ineffectiveness; that is, it will point out that duration is of no consequence to the situation, that all remains the same, that writing and reading are repetitious and in that sense abolish time.

The image of the pigeon crossing the sun on page 3 is reiterated to indicate a new beginning on page 25: "Yellow then black then yellow again, the body itself, in the rapid vertical ascent reduced to a line."[3] The pigeon has become an arrow, and we are reminded of the epigraph, where the sun and therefore time are immobile. The idea of nonduration arises from the contrast between the rapidly moving black line across the sun, which does suggest the passage of time, and the repetition of the event itself, indicating that *no time* has elapsed between its first description and its second one.[4] As the observer's eyes lift to the window across the street, he notices "the bulging shape of the cloud creeping from one frame to the other" (4). On page 24, immediately preceding the pigeon's flight, the cloud still drifts across the windowpane: ". . . the right side of the window seemed to move the reflection of the cloud shifting. . . ."

These first twenty-five pages contain all the principal elements that the rest of the novel will elaborate. They represent an initial, unsuccessful development, akin perhaps to a trial run, but also, in terms of our present concern with time, the initial repetition from which are born subsequent ones, itself born of the last lines of the novel in unending circularity. Real time has been abolished, its representation undermined through the self-negating reappearance of recognizable time indicators (e.g., pigeon across sun, and cloud). Thus, in the title of the last part of the novel "Chronology of events," Chronology does not bear its accustomed meaning, but refers rather to narrative sequence per se, and events not to narrated circumstance but to circumstance *as* narrated.

Such a drastic transformation of normal fictional coordinates also affects the traditional manifestations of point of view. While we have spoken of an "observer," his identity is by no means well defined, although he remains the same in his capacity as a recorder. These shifts in the center of consciousness are not new in Simon. The narrator of *The Flanders Road,* for instance, could see himself as *je* and *il;* likewise, in *The Palace,* he cannot adopt an objective stance towards "the student," while in *Histoire* he freely identifies with his Uncle Charles.

II *Alternative Visions, Alternative Journeys*

The very concept of point of view and the options it offers becomes in *The Battle of Pharsalus* a means of self-examination by the narrative. Just as language is shown to be on an immediate level but one representational alternative—the other ones contained by it through description being, in particular, sculpture, painting, and film—so does point of view undergo its initial questioning through being transposed into its equivalents in those other modes. Illumination, painting, and engraving are seen as alternate instruments of figuration. These options are introduced at moments when a chosen mode of perception (e.g., sound) appears unequal to its task, particularly near the central scene of the narration, the assumed or imagined coitus between the observer's mistress and the red-haired man. Listening behind the closed door, the narrator wishes for a "seeing ear" (13). The text then moves on to other possibilities of "illuminating" a scene—"The shaft of another spotlight suddenly shifted leaped from one member of the audience to another... (13)[5]—or of seizing it—"... the point of the nail or the knife which made them had torn off in passing across the thin layer of paint tiny scales..." (14). These determinations appear as the result of a contradictory desire for more complete knowledge of what his ear cannot see, as well as for greater objectivity: the cold detachment of the light technician, perhaps, or of the anonymous inscribers of graffiti.

Comparable transitions to supposedly more impersonal and more revealing artistic media take place throughout the fiction at similar moments of impotent jealousy. The narrator, in his guise as Uncle Charles, observes the artist Van Velden at work: "I watched the brush take a little geranium pink then a gob of white..." (30). The two friends are in the midst of a heated argument about Charles's mistress, whom he suspects of deceiving him. Near the end of the first part, the sequence, from helpless jealousy to alternate instrument of representation, has been welded into a single thought: "seeing ear the brush still advancing toward the right" (57).

In the last section of Part II, entitled "O," the presence of the observer and that of the object under scrutiny are both studied, in an effort to make an objecive analysis of the situation, which becomes also an ironic statement on the oft examined problems of narrative point of view. The problem, apparently simple as first given, soon becomes increasingly complicated, while an attempt to include all pertinent variables of the situation ultimately render it as elusive as ever. The section opens with the clarity and forcefulness that accompanies most beginnings, "Begin again, start over from zero. Let O be the position occupied by the eye of the observer (O.)" (123), and ends with the description of a variable mobile scheme of ever changing contour and minimal fixities: "... we must represent the totality of the system as a moving body ceaselessly altering around a few fixed points, for example the intersection of the line OO with the trajectory of the pigeon in flight, or again that of the itineraries of two journeys, or again the name PHARSALUS figuring in a Latin textbook and disfigured on a signpost beside a road in Thessaly" (127). In this system, the observer also becomes the object of observation. The axis along which the activity is engaged in may be fixed or mobile, and so may its goal and origin. The possibilities for actual transformation of the point of view once established, the text will undertake to illustrate this development in Part III, where O (the letter stands for observer, object, apex of angle of vision, etc.)[6] can be the initial consciousness with which the novel began, or Charles as a young man and as a father, or the deceitful woman, unfaithful to O in both its male identities. Consistent with a variable focus, the fiction's central sequence will itself be subjected to a number of modifications. It is at the end of this main sequence that we find the "moving body" in the above quote; it concludes several journeys which constitute the general pattern of the novel and that of its individual parts, as the preceding quotation also implies. Important manifestations of this repeated journey are already presented in the first twenty-five pages which constitute a thematic introduction: on page 25 the restatement of the very first line of the narrative (yellow, etc.) clearly begins a new development. Simon himself confirms this view of the first pages and calls them "a short prelude where the different themes ... are briefly exposed."[7]

Three principal journeys take place in the first segment of the novel. The first figurative one is simply the trajectory of the observer's glance toward the fifth-floor window, together with all that is in his angle of vision, "the cone represented ... by the angle TOF" (124), where T is the curb in front of the building across the street and F is the window. The eye repeatedly encounters the blank windowpane. The initial vision of the pigeon across the sun draws the eye to the window, and according to Ricardou becomes, as an elaboration of the epigraph, the source of the entire first part ("Achilles running motionless"). Besides this development, there are three more attempts to penetrate, as it were, beyond the blank windowpanes. The last one itself comprises three successive moments. Each attempt gathers erotic momentum from elements it encounters along the visual path. Points along the trajectory closest to the vacant window are in general more sexually suggestive than the rest, in anticipation of the scene inside. Such allusions, however, remain as yet relatively mild. The main stages along the way to the window are: people emerging from a subway exit (initially counted in Arabic numerals, then written numbers), the youths at the café across the street, some pigeons. The window slowly acquires some life: first as a cloud drifts across it, then in the suspected movement of the curtains. The last transition draws the observer inside the building: "Pretend to get into an invisible pair of trousers then pull them up to your waist. The V and the A replaced by What do you call them: ideograms? LA MAISON DU ♥ESTON ET DU PΛNTΛLON. Laid. Get yourself laid. The expression for women too. Sure of hearing muffled noises behind the door when he knocked" (11). One can easily see how the idea of *enfiler un pantalon* ("get into your trousers") together with that of "ideograms" whose argot correlatives, that is to say, whose corresponding concepts at the argot level of thinking are sexual graffiti, naturally leads to *se faire grimper* ("get yourself laid"; *enfiler* is another argot equivalent of *grimper*).

The second important form of the journey takes place inside the building. The previous trajectory included all the elements belonging to the sweep of a glance (TOF); similarly, this one will encompass the entire visible setting, and transform its various elements into specific stages along its path. Further, whereas the previous journey was principally tied to vision, this one will depend more particularly on writing or drawing. As we saw, it was introduced by the idea of graffiti. The attempt to learn what is happening in the room occurs three times in this sequence, the last one also becoming a series of three repeated assaults, the verbal equivalent of physically charging the door. The stages along this path are: a leaking faucet, the scored walls of the corridor, the closed door. Each attempt also comes closer to penetrating inside the room or to visualizing clearly the love-making within; as before, the elements of the journey each offer possibilities for erotic development. The drops of water from the faucet, for instance, appear to draw a hairy line suggestive of pubic hair. Here also, the last attempt provides the bridge to the next aspect of the journey, as the final collage of sexual imagery compares the erected penis to a Roman soldier's pilum. The paragraph that follows, although it returns to the description of the café table's surface, expands it at the end to introduce other inscribed surfaces in the form of the titles of various studies on the Battle of Pharsalus, continuing the implications of the penis-pilum comparison. We note further that the choice of texts pertaining to the battle is the exact counterpart of the preceding moment, in this sense: the markings and scars on the café table, as well as those on the walls of the corridor, are external to the scene inside the room, whose exact configuration has not been described, not yet adequately visualized. They characterize the surroundings of the still largely blank event. Similarly, the texts in question concern contingent aspects of the Battle of Pharsalus having to do precisely with the mere terrain: *"the topographical and tactical theory* of this battle has given rise to several hypotheses . . ." (15).

The third journey sequence of the introductory pages is situated in Greece where the narrator and Nikos, his companion, are searching for the battlefield of Pharsalus. Although this is in fact a true voyage, it corresponds in its principal stages to the dominant moments of the metaphorical journeys that we have examined, and it is in its turn divisible into three attempts. The situation at the beginning of this journey is similar to that of the first one ("visual" trajectory): there is a group of people at a café table whom the protagonist does not understand. In the previous case, the main cause of this incomprehension was distance: the young people were across the street; their gestures remained mysterious. Here, the language is a barrier; the narrator needs his friend Nikos, presumably a Greek, to interpret directions. The attempts to find the battlefield are unsuccessful; the scene at the conclusion of each try is an empty field, filled by O's memories of a war experience or by the broken-down hulk of a mechanical harvester; stages along the path to the site of the battle correspond to those met by the glance to the window, or the progress in the corridor toward the door. Greek newspapers and signposts are the present graffiti. A Shell station, or a café, echoes the previous café and the hallway's faucet. But the scene of the battle remains unfound, the lovemaking couple ill-defined. Although this journey contains within it, and consistently alludes to, all the previously suggestive elements of its predecessors, the text is as yet incapable of filling the central void. The entire thematic introduction ends with the observer once more glancing at the fifth-floor window, and a comment to his companion back at Pharsala: "you're right it takes us nowhere we'll go back where we started maybe this time we" (25). This is in effect what happens as the narrative returns to the opening image and begins anew.

By situating them at the conclusion of corresponding trajectories, the text has so far established the metaphorical equivalence of the Battle of Pharsalus, the love scene, the narrator's memories of World War II, and the disabled farming machine. As yet, none of these concluding designs is described in great detail, for the narrative does not possess enough material from which to fashion them. Indeed, each one of the journeys is an effort to "create" the Battle of Pharsalus, or its counterparts, and the entire novel will pursue this interest in a rhythm of invention closely parallel to that of this introductory passage. (The number three, for instance, will continue to prevail. We have seen until now three forms of the quest; the first one ended at the window, the second one at the door, the third one in the Greek countryside. Each one of these quests comprises three distinct repetitions, the last of which is itself divisible into three moments.)

Two basic ideas may further be discerned from our examination of these pages: first, the journey may be likened to a voyage of atonement, a species of pilgrimage; secondly, we are witnessing in all these attempts not only the effort to create the Battle of Pharsalus, the "Holy Site," as it were, but also the effort to create the instrument or vehicle of the pilgrimage, the necessary language, since it is ultimately a verbal voyage.

The expiatory overtones of O's endeavor, though they are introduced by religious imagery, do not themselves have an exclusively religious intent, and when they do, it is either ironic or frankly critical. Christian symbolism appears in the first pages, but is clearly subverted to the specific needs of the text; a transition from the triangle of the Trinity to that of the vulva is typical of the general direction that obeisance takes in the narrative, while it offers a return to the very source of the religious symbol itself. Birds in general, pigeons, doves are linked with the sexual embrace, rather than with the Holy Spirit. The idea of a pilgrimage is maintained because of the religious origins of the imagery, while this imagery is used in a profane context. Thus, the people climbing to the street from the subway are compared to a catechism picture where the faithful are ascending into the clouds, following the hand of a woman imperiously pointing towards heaven. This hand in its turn becomes the arrow that shows the way to the public underground lavatories, the corridors of limbo or hell.

The double import of such figurations, when linked to Charles, transforms him into a Januslike figure whose intercession opens the doors to a dubious paradise: "... he was always sitting under the yellowish glow of the electric bulb, like a sort of funereal figure ..." (8). Workers are waiting along the corridor for their pay, "a kind of food or viaticum they had come to receive from his hand, the coins that used to be slipped into the mouths of those who had to pay their passage across" (8). It is precisely with this very image that O's itinerary around Pharsala begins; he asks his friend for some aspirin; the men around the café tables remind him of those waiting at his uncle's door, and both ideas then merge in an echo of the previous metaphor: "what viaticum in their mouths? Salty taste of the brass on the tongue" (15). During the trip O confesses the reason for wanting to see the battlefield: "But it's because of that assignment ..." (18). He will need two more aspirin tablets, his viaticum, before deciding to start the search once more from the beginning, after straying for the third time.

This particular voyage to Pharsala, and by extension the entire novel, is seen by him as an effort to redeem himself as regards his dead uncle. The first mention of Charles in the book appears in the context of the old photograph of Van Velden's studio and the second refers to the impression his death left on O. These two constants remain primordial throughout the novel, and inseparable, because of the very indivisibility of love and death. The photograph provides initial material for the birth of jealousy and the memory of Charles's death, itself linked to the Battle of Pharsalus and to death in general; it completes the circle by relating jealousy with lovemaking, lovemaking with war, war with death and love, and so on. The trip contains the principal elements of the novel; the whole narration is itself a journey of discovery, creation, and abolition. Once more we see as one of the purposes of narrative the effort to comprehend and contain through language some previously misunderstood situation, a liberating endeavor. By re-creating and understanding a possible drama of his uncle's life, O expects to free himself from the bonds of his present ignorance.

III *Necessary Words*

O's concept of his unawareness is intimately connected with his knowledge of language. His effort to explain the past necessitates that he learn a new tongue, and if we conceive this explanation as a re-creation, the language will have to be created ex nihilo. Along the way to the center of the mystery he encounters people whom he does not understand: the young men across the street, the Greeks, later some Spaniards on a train.

Continuously, when the narration enters into a moment of stress—that is to say, when the "charged" vocabulary accumulates previously distinct segments of narrative—there appear realizations of ignorance accompanied generally by admissions of suffering and a new awareness of the power of death (also linking the triad jealousy-love-death). This is so, for instance, in the introductory section of the novel, during the recalled remonstrance by his uncle concerning his ignorance of language, where "I didn't yet know" (9) is repeated, and there are statements about death in various guises: "Dead secret Living dead," "dead wood dead leaf," "dead tired death penalty" (9).[8] These words appear in normal script, while his uncle's comments, which they interrupt, are given in italics, as if they were part of an extraneous text.[9] They represent O's present answer to Charles's assertions at that moment that he needed to learn the use of words: *"but perhaps you're right after all knowing everything never leads to anything but learning something more and words lead to other words ..."* (9); for the fiction is O's acknowledgement of his ignorance and his creation of a needed vocabulary. That is why at the beginning we find the greatest number of ideograms standing out in the text as islands of nonverbal significance, waiting to be resolved into words. These ideograms at the same time represent, in terms of the novel as a total graffito, the counterpart of the individual examples of graffiti which appear at various points on O's itinerary. The use of ciphers instead of written numbers is also part of this "birth of language," although it belongs as well to other patterns of correspondence (such as the parallelism between the crowd emerging from the subway and the armies at Pharsalus).

The ideograms will be used as representations of the central, not as yet clarified, elements of the narrative. The first one is the pointing hand. It soon undergoes its simplification to become an arrow. Considering the novel a sequence of repeated itineraries, the importance of this sign becomes clear, and its appearance as the first unresolved sign indicates that the direction of the journey is to be the primary problem. It will never be quite resolved, any more than the central mystery will be totally clarified. The arrow reappears near the end of the novel, marking the resurgence of the question and pointing at the same time to the circularity of the narrative. The second hieroglyph is contained in the capitalized name of a clothier's establishment, (see p. 11), where the V becomes a drawing of two lapels and the A two trousered legs. These designs are also quickly stylized into Λ and V to represent the enigma at the end of the journey: V as the vulva, Λ, which stood for the legs of a man, as the penis; together they are an ideographic transcription of the imagined copulation. They may likewise be resolved into arrows pointing upwards and downwards to suggest again that the ultimate problem is one of direction, that of finding the true itinerary, at the end of which the quest will be completed. Hence they are also indicators of the initial direction of this quest, that of the visual trajectory of O, up to the window and down to the street and the subway exit. They will reappear near the end to mark the return of the unsolved mystery, corollaries of the arrow that points to a new beginning.

At the outset of the broad development of the novel, after the introductory section, there appears the ideogram for a shirt, folded. The drawing can be abstracted into its components as a square, i.e., four arrows pointing in four directions. The sketch of the shirt is preceded by a passage about Charles in which memories of the odor of fermented grapes in his office suggest to O a permanent aura of death. It is followed by the description of an eviscerated bird, used to discover signs of the future. The passage must be considered a tentative, drastic resolution of the enigma by killing it, or refusing it. In effect, Charles, the source of the investigation and its reason, is seen as dead even in life; and for the first time in the narration, birds, associated with sex, and therefore, also the goal of the quest, are killed in a premature negation of the riddle. The ideogram thus offers, resolves, and discards the question posed by the arrows pointing in all directions. It alludes to O's first reaction to the magnitude of the task ahead.

The elements so far examined remain basic throughout the novel. The essential vocabulary now acquired is put to use towards an exact description of the "battle" (or its alternate forms: sex, machine, translation, etc.), whose importance in the text will be proportionally greater than the stages of the journey towards it, until this latter factor regains its importance in Part III. As the battle now comes directly into play, its descriptions are more certain: the transcript of translated Latin text is followed by a portion of O's own corrected version. It is at this point that the temptation to consider the problem to be worked out suggests itself, with the thought of O's uncle's living in death and of the shirt ideogram. But an erotic image gives new impetus to the language, and previously vague incidents become clear. A youth leaning over the café table, considered earlier "perhaps ... drunk" (4), is declared a "drunkard" (28). Gestures of the waiter addressed to the group of young people are understood to be a reprimand; the window on the fifth floor is half open. The passages that follow all point to a minimization of the enigma: Van Velden[10] scolds O for transforming an unimportant erotic adventure into tragedy; O admits that his attraction for the woman is akin to his fascination with vulgarity and the delights of guilt. But the idea of guilt introduces once more the difficult Latin translation, replete with its mystery, and the cycle begins anew. At this point the battle permeates the text, finding reinforcement in all the elements which previously surrounded it. Alternative situations that are its correlatives are developed, and by their proximity to the central scene are "polarized" to become effectively its substitutes. Eventually they all lead to the door at the end of the corridor. These surrogate battles are: (1) the text of the "Battle of Pharsalus"; (2) the translation by O; (3) a soccer match

seen on the way to the Pharsalus battlefield; (4) O's personal
experience during World War II; (5) a riotous student procession in Paris; (6) three frames of a comic strip in the newspaper; (7) the memory of a drunken soldier in the barracks;
(8) the McCormick harvester. All are themselves reinforced by
other elements of the "vocabulary"[11] which also have acquired
significant sexual connotations, or which signal the proximity of
the central mystery: birds in general, the windowpanes, clouds,
water, the water tap, or the Shell gas station; also statements
such as "I didn't know," "I suffered"; the corridor, graffiti in
general, marks of any sort, signs, dogs (Kynos Kephalai was
itself a battle[12]; the lovers in the room are seen as "crestfallen
dogs stuck together" [p. 14]), a man and a woman loading hay.

Other details are continuously infused with sexual or violent
connotations as the narrative develops, adding to the "lexicon"
and diminishing the segments of erotically inert prose. The central scene and its alternate forms are first interrupted by frequent
returns to the original observation point or to portions of the
Greek trip. But their mutual attraction and the effect of intensifying detail recall them with increasing frequency until they
fuse into an uninterrupted sequence where all these scenes, or
aspects of them, are either implied or restated; the whole passage is dominated by two corresponding segments: O's race
against death, a personal episode of World War II; and his
furious pounding at the door of the silent room. The breathless
anxiety of these two events flows from one to the other until
the door becomes an obstacle to O's survival, while on the railroad track (ie., corridor) where he is running, the breathless-
ness results more from jealousy than exhaustion. At this moment,
jealousy, death and love are indissolubly linked. Having reached
an apex of connotative tension, the text reaches outside of itself
to include aspects of "transformed" elements: a line from the
epigraph, "Achilles running motionless" (56), and two short
passages from Proust. As is the case almost invariably in the
sequences describing aspects of the battle, this one ends with
the image of a penis in the act of penetration and the words
"I was suffering like" (57).

This summit of intensity is followed by a gradual quiescence,
a downward curve of diminishing personal involvement with,

or subjection to, the text on O's part. Except for occasional outbursts, such as "redheaded son of a whore" (58), the images now described slowly recede from the vortex of action. Although an external quote is introduced (from *The Golden Ass*) in the hope that its highly erotic content may flag the text into renewed activity, the latter has literally drained itself, and the downward movement continues. The "vocabulary" is thoroughly voided of its generative possibilities: "now there are no more pigeons on the square" (63); "there was no longer anyone," "the cafe terrace is empty" (64). More decisively still, even though some activity and all its latent content reappears, they allow for no development: "a couple has come out onto the terrace"; "There is nothing particularly" (65).

IV   *The Syntax of Allusion*

The second part of the novel, entitled "Lexicon," deals with themes introduced in the first part and, according to Simon, "elaborated with variations separately one after the other, in the second part; Battle, Warrior, Machine, Caesar, Voyage, O finally."[13] As the title indicates, the role of this section is to create a final lexicon in preparation for the effort of discovery or invention in the last part. The conclusion of Part I saw the language weakened and incapable of giving impetus to any new attack upon the closed door or of inventing a clearer delineation of the mystery. The reappraisal undertaken now of some important elements will be characterized by a systematic effort to maintain objectivity, though it be threatened on all sides by each new consideration or variable introduced into the system. Such is the development of the section entitled "O," whose attempt to objectify the entire enterprise offers the most obvious illustration of a prevailing pattern.

"O" starts with an enjoinment to himself, by the observer-narrator, to begin anew, start, appropriately enough, from point zero. Soon, however, the mathematical model he erects begins to lose its precision, to allow subjectivity, in the guise of metaphor, to creep in and undermine it. Having defined as a cone the field of vision encompassed by O in his observation of the window and the sidewalk in front of him, the system begins to break down with the consideration of what *does not* belong to it: ". . . O,

for instance, not actually seeing the three pigeons which, seeking food (seeds or rubbish left by the market set up here in
the morning?) describe on the pavement vague meanders ..."
(124). The birds insert: (1) the idea of defining what *is seen*
in terms of what is *not seen*; (2) mobility; (3) the erotic connotations which they have accumulated throughout the narrative; (4) the unnecessary consideration of peripheral matter; (5)
the opportunity for language to free itself of temporary bonds
and create its own sequence.

This sequence now controls the text, elaborating an ever
widening metaphor that opens the door for some of the most
emotionally charged elements of the previous pages. At this
point the observer tries to regain control: "Start over, organize.
First, second, third" (125). It is a vain effort; a bird reenters
the field of vision, and its flight, "yellow, black crossbow, then
yellow again" (125), across the window establishes the necessity of considering the latter a possible point of observation,
in its turn, whose object would then be O himself. The identity
of the new observer, at first uncertain as to gender, becomes
finally feminine. The number of alternatives now grows, O is
"merely a simple point included within any other cone of vision
sweeping the square" (126), and when the original O acquires
mobility, "O moving rapidly from one place to another the
world appears at no moment identical" (127), we are led to
consider the scheme a constantly moving system with no fixed
points of reference, a temporary equilibrium sustained by
language.

The attempt to impose an external order on the intrinsic tendencies of language is constantly thwarted. One of the basic
patterns of the novel arises from this continuous struggle between the desire for one particular kind of order on the part
of O, and the apparent willfulness of words seeking their own
continuity. Initial organization is slowly sapped to reach moments of seeming anarchy where punctuation disappears, and
the scission between the two forces at work in the narrative is
so pronounced that entire paragraphs interpose themselves into
the flow of narration, to create two separate sequences. This
opposition generally arises when any of the five contingencies, listed above with regard to the pigeons, is present.

The first segment of the second part, "Battle," aptly illustrates this pattern. Forced to deal with the movement inherent in the matter at hand, which after all is a battle, the narrator attempts to create a modicum of order by trying to situate the battle at some particular time of day. Erotic connotations and the inevitable mobility of action transform early calm into a final unrestrained accumulation of imagery. Occasional efforts to fixate the text by passing from the description of action to that of its representation in painting, for instance, prove fruitless, merely allowing the movement of the represented event to transfer itself to the text, giving it an extra dimension of mobility: we have a proliferation of transitions from depiction of action to depiction of painted action, to the intrusion of extranovelistic passages. Any attempt to situate in time is finally discarded: "no longer time no morning no night time stopped no yesterday no last year ten years ago today" (81). Battle scenes alternate with erotic ones and with all their previously established substitutes (soccer match, World War II experience, etc.). The only functioning time has become the present of narration: "now he leaps forward," "now the short piece of arrow," "now she puts her arms around his shoulders," "now two little girls" (82–83). It is the very axis of organization chosen at the outset, time, that has been most greatly subverted, requiring as an alternative structure a complete reliance on language proper.

As we pointed out, from the pattern of this subversion arises the complex orchestration that creates one of the structural bonds of the novel. It links in Part II, for instance, the first and last segments, "Battle" (no. 1) and "O" (no. 7), as failed attempts to impose two of the most pervasive and usually stringent types of order on the flow of language: spatial ("O") and temporal ("Battle"). Similar affinities bind "Caesar" (no. 2) and "Voyage" (no. 6) as well as "Conversation" (no. 3) and "Machine" (no. 5).

"Caesar" represents an effort to diminish the hold of the presiding "divinity" at the Battle of Pharsalus; that is to say, Caesar himself in the context of his relationship to the significance of that historical event in the novel, and Uncle Charles in terms of his own relationship to the novel, *The Battle of Pharsalus*. The chapter deals first with a pilgrimage to Lourdes, an under-

taking parallel to the narrator's own journeys in the narrative.
The image chosen to suggest the idea of pilgrimage in the first
part (viaticum, wafer, aspirin) is also introduced here: "the
Host during the Elevation" (85–86). The narrator's grandmother
was at that time the mythical presence whose mystery is partially revealed to him, as she unbuttons her dress to reach for
banknotes that are to provide the tip to the bellboy. The text
moves in several stages from her to Charles, to the Battle of
Pharsalus, and to Caesar. The opening moment is similar to
that at the beginning of all other journeys: the narrator is at
a disadvantage, in a situation whose ramifications he does not
understand. Here he does not know exactly what is happening:
"after a murmured exchange of words with Maman" (84). A
mystery is revealed to him; his grandmother's action deprives her
somewhat of her previous stature. This revelation proves to be
disillusioning: grandmother's breast holds, among her jewelry,
"those filthy wrinkled papers with their grayish or earthen colors,
exhaling an indefinable odor of mildew" (86). The revelation
is in its turn linked with Uncle Charles and his own distribution
of salaries to workers who resembled the innumerable sick,
crippled, and dying at Lourdes: "inseparable from that bloody
and omnipresent background bristling with nails, spines, lances
and guarded by black groups of centurions cast in bronze"
(86). The transition is thus effected to the Battle of Pharsalus
and thereby, to Caesar himself, his mythic reality now diminished.

The movement from the hotel room to Caesar takes place
in three principal stages, a development also followed by
"Voyage," where the transition is provided by a train stop
when three passengers (Spaniards: incomprehension) leave to
be replaced by two new ones (a young woman, a man: erotic
potential). The episode concludes with scenes where O's jealous
obsession (or Charles's) and the idea of death (Battle) are
ridiculed: once more Van Velden suggests that the woman is
not worth O's worry; the narrator himself imagines the foolish
death of someone who opens a door leading off the train, believing it is the door to the toilet. However, both concerns
remain. "Conversation" and "Machine" expand previously introduced elements, also with the intention of diminishing the

sexual content of the central vision, trying to create two new entries in the lexicon. The scene elaborated in "Conversation" is that in which Van Velden's wife announces that her husband is not in. In this instance, she persuades O to remain. He comes to realize that she is herself preoccupied with her husband's relationship with his model and expects O to give her information. He leaves with his opinion of Van Velden and his wife lessened, though not his jealousy. "Machine" is the expansion of one of the substitute elements of the Battle of Pharsalus, the McCormick harvester previously encountered at the end of one journey. It is here described in detail, in an attempt to "empty" it also of its implications, but the description remains what it was before, an alternative for the vision of lovemaking: "...the energy transmitted from the axle of the wheels to the various parts was then transformed into either rotating movements ... or ... alternating back-and-forth movements ..." (103).

The central segment of Part II, "Warrior," owes its situation to the fact that all jealous emotion in the narrative concentrates upon the oft reviled "redheaded son of a whore" whose figure haunts O's mind. He is here described as a drink-crazed, red-haired veteran soldier, whose initially ridiculous appearance slowly grows in stature, so that he becomes at the end a tragic figure worthy of respect. Once more the desire of the narrator to impose a private form upon his material has been diverted by the material's acquired momentum.

Rather than creating a malleable medium, the effort in Part II to erase the connotations of language has once more given it the opportunity to assert its dominion. In this context Part III represents a necessary development in the pattern of the novel, the final stage of the battle. The first forty pages introduced the material. The rest of Part I undertook to examine it from the inside, as it were, relying on the implication of the observer, his readiness to assume with equal effectiveness a variety of points of view. But the language created and developed in this manner acquired sufficient power to subvert the activity of the narrating consciousness, if not to fill the absence at the center (sexual scene, battle). We remain at the periphery of the Battle of Pharsalus (topography). Part II attempted to isolate important elements of the "conflict" and to analyze them in terms of their relationship with the narrator, to impose from without a reliable framework (temporal, spatial, visual). There remained a duality in the text: the central consciousness, although itself multi-faceted, was distinguishable from the material it dealt with. Yet its position was greatly weakened, at the mercy of the greater power acquired by the narration at its expense. It only remained to abolish this distance and transform the focus of vision into one more element in the pattern of language, a development already begun in the segment "O" of Part II.

V *The Absence Within*

With this in mind, we realize that the objectivity of Part III is but a reflection of the greater freedom gained by the components of the narrative, rather than the reverse. We have not an omniscient point of view, but an omniscient linguistic structure, a self-organizing text, which functions almost exclusively in the present tense of the written word. This is why it is most clear in this part that O's persona adopts several masks, and can be the woman in the coitus as well as the deceived lover. And at the conclusion of the novel, it is O who sits at a table with some of the elements that the narrative has left behind as its residue: a package of Gauloises (wings, Vercingétorix, Caesar), a scallop shell (Shell station, travel), a Larousse, and himself, with the sun on a white sheet of paper. For the circularity of the structure arises out of the situation in which O is implicated, rather than from his own activity.[14]

Upon considering segment "O" of Part II, we noted that, as an instance, the anticipated intrusion of a bird into the field of vision begins the breakdown of the geometrical organization. That is to say, the system must be transformed in terms of the contingencies of the point of view (of O's presence as a starting point) and their growth into ever widening metaphor. These contingencies are easily encompassed by the text as it incorporates them, together with O their point of origin. Now that language flows unimpeded we may expect to discover the basic relationships previously disturbed, a condition aptly summarized in the third epigraph by Heidegger and quoted here in part: "The tool turns out to be damaged or the material unsuitable. . . .

When its unusability is thus discovered, equipment becomes conspicuous . . ." (129). By "tool" we understand O:[15] the "discovering" is the task performed by this last part of the novel.

The central enigma of the first two parts of the novel does not resist the creative impetus of an unconditional text. The door that stood in O's way is no obstacle now: the action is seen from within. Language gives this scene full expression and repeats it; it also permits all its substitute renditions to appear as they are beckoned. No longer a danger, eroticism and its alternates (battles, machine) permeate the narrative, following a rising curve of intensity until the battle is over. At the end, however, the central problem has not been solved, simply bypassed through the displacement of O and his subjectivity; its central manifestation subsides, quiescent among the ruins, waiting perhaps to resume its role: "Lying flat on the ground among the capitals of the broken columns and the architrave fragments, the two interlaced figures with stone entrails . . . the silent murmur of their blood, the imperceptible shudder of their breathing, the mineral trace of their forms recall their existence" (185–186).

The dangers inherent in a subjective attempt to define a field of vision, which lead to examining the limits of what must be encompassed through a consideration of what is absent, afford an apt illustration of the transformations undergone by the narrative in its third part. Accounts of what is not directly perceived remain within the confines of the action described without allowing it to proliferate. Thus, in the first "take" of the lovemaking scene: "They cannot hear the sound of the drop falling at regular intervals from the faucet at the end of the corridor" (155). Later, in the same scene described as a bas-relief: "The contour of the woman's body, although broken and splintered in places, still appears in its entirety (the eye supplying the missing sections) . . ." (185). Significantly, these are the only two instances where the nonperceivable is introduced, in moments of high erotic content, displaying the containing power of the description through such straining at its limits.

Mobility, which previously introduced numerous, unexpected contingencies in the narrator's vision, has similarly been integrated. It is transformed into the movement inherent in a description as opposed to its object, that is, the transition from descriptions of action to descriptions of stillness and vice versa. Scenes of great animation, for instance, are easily restrained, since to a large extent they derive initially from other representations, such as paintings. They may be animated, pressed into action, so to speak, by the text, and then returned to their original stasis. This occurs in the case of (1) the naked warrior, (2) the erotic scene (slowly transformed into a sculpture), and (3) the flight during the more recent war (also becoming a bas-relief). The limits of the text's power of containment are tested in this manner, particularly with regard to the ubiquitous "naked warrior": "This figure is borrowed from a composition by Polidoro da Caravaggio. The left side, left arm and left hand are pressed against the top of the heavy table . . . In a few seconds the entire left side of the naked body will be soiled with gray dust through which drops of blood will gradually seep" (168). In effecting the transition from Caravaggio's study to the drunken soldier, the future penetrates. The appearance of future tenses in a pervasive present (it occurs one other time in a similar scene) signals the resisting core of mystery, that is, the identity of the "other man." Efforts to eliminate the unknown factor result in the repeated (three times) description of the drawing, with, in each case, an exact reiteration of the statement: "This figure is borrowed from a composition by Polidoro da Caravaggio."

The vortex of activity of Part III remains the lovemaking sequence and its adjoining elements, from the closest (the naked warrior) to those seemingly most remote from it in content or connotation (a street demonstration). It appears four times in this section, in great detail, each time introduced by those factors which we have learned to recognize as its preludes or corollaries (pigeon, window, flight from death, machine). It too almost forces the narration out of its objective boundaries.

The reverberations of this scene are felt throughout the text: there are no erotically neutral passages left. Components which previously marked the itinerary to this event are now saturated with its connotations in such a way that the entire third part, save perhaps the first paragraph, seems composed of alternate renditions of the coupling. There is, nevertheless, a noticeable rise in intensity leading to its first full account (147–148). The main points of its prelude are as follows: (1) two young boys play a sexual game near the harvesting machine; (2) laborers are seen digging a trench, bare-chested; (3) bare-chested men and women rise from tombs; (4) a street demonstration amasses in front of a barracks; (5) a pigeon flies across the half-opened fifth-floor window. The erotic episode follows.

In a previous description of the moment where O meets the young model who, presumably, will become his mistress, she is described at length, the paragraph ending with: "... her open mouth. Inside can be seen her pink tongue." (138). This first relation of the completed coitus is interrupted on similar words: "The smile exposes her teeth between which appears the pink tip of her tongue." (148). The text takes advantage of a previously established rhythm to interrupt the situation and shift to a more controllable one, which consists of a detailed description of the people arising through a subway exit, (parallel to that of (3) above). But the pressure to pursue the incomplete passage continues. The last woman coming out of the subway is trying to close a basket whose cover keeps rising "about forty-five degrees" (p. 149). She leaves, her back bowed. On these faint suggestions of sex—forty-five degrees: "the stiffened penis" (147); bowed back: "The body leaning over her" (p. 147)—and the image of bursting fullness (both of the text and the man's penis), the coitus continues until the movement of the bodies ceases as the couple hear someone (O) outside the door. Once again the break occurs at a moment already established. (The journey sequences to the door ceased at this point.) The transitionary paragraphs introduce moments of lesser erotic content, as before, although they are now simply alternate renditions of the coitus, aspects of the crucial battle: we see the end of the manifestation from the point of view of the soldiers, the conversation between O's friend and the Greeks, a truck raising a cloud of dust over the road's "potholes" (French: *nids de poule*) (152). The conclusion of the demonstration was intended as an alternate subsidence to the incomplete embrace. But the military uniforms introduce the discussion about the Battle of Pharsalus and a sequel, the truck on the Pharsala road. Two elements of the truck's advance are excep-

tionally sensitized: the cloud of dust (cf. clouds across the
window at the beginning); and the *nids de poule*, with their
suggestion of birds. These two elements are expanded by the
following paragraph, although there is an effort to "objectify
them": the cloud's appearance is rendered in terms reminiscent
of a physics problem, where the suggestive contents of the
truck—"cosmetics and Beauty Aids or Articles for Dowries and
Weddings" (36)—are eliminated: "Raised by a moving body
(no more than a point) proceeding horizontally, a streak of dust
advances along the foot of the hill" (152). Similarly, the birds
are seen in terms of their rectilinear flight, their harsh cry.

Nevertheless, this is sufficient to cause the insertion of a scene
even closer to the center: O is translating the passage on the
Battle of Pharsalus. His uncle, this time, approves. The assignment is successful because the text has successfully achieved
the alternate scene to the battle, the coitus. The translation is
interrupted by a return to the flight of the birds: they are now
flying in gradually ascending planes, an indication of the
influence exerted by the intervening lines. The scene that follows
is that of O's flight in World War II, at whose last interrupted
moment, when O's heart is pounding, the love scene reenters:
"His blood is pounding and roaring in his ears. Motionless the
man and the woman hear their blood pounding through their
veins..." (p. 155). It continues until perspiration cools on the
immobile bodies. After an interval in which each paragraph
marks an even closer approximation to the central scene, the
latter is repeated, the wording exactly the same, except for
the elimination of two sentences on the noise behind the door.
This suppression of two short sentences marks a tightening of
the previous rendition through the discarding of peripheral
matter. At the same time, it points to the further diminution
of O's role (first narrator) in the development of the text, in
anticipation of his presence at the end as another variable in
the structure. Indeed, the change in this exact transcription finds
its counterpart in two incidents involving the McCormick harvester: first, two men arrive in a small truck and take some parts
away; then, an old man breaks off a board on which is painted
the trademark. For the first time, we find out that some letters
of the name were missing, that, in fact, one could only read

MC OR ICK. The further dilapidation of this close surrogate of the central scene reflects, then, what has happened in the text already (not quite an exact transcription) and anticipates other attacks upon it. Also, it informs us that previous readings of the situation were incorrect (the name was given as complete); the correction has begun with regard to the machine, and with regard to the erotic episode (diminution of the intruder's role). Lastly, it points to the very manner of the final attack: the writing will effect a gradual breaking up of the incident. In effect, near the end, it is progressively transformed into an ancient sculpture (see above), which has been left incomplete but which one recognizes "(The eye supplying the missing sections)."

As previously observed, the fixation of the central scene is not final. Amid the stones remains an "imperceptible shudder" and as an indication of the still latent possibilities of the text, its urge to start anew, two basic ideograms of the beginning make their reappearance near the end:

ᐯESTON ET DU PΛNTΛLON.

This and other echoes of the first pages suggest in this novel also the circularity that is one aspect of the necessary rereading.

CHAPTER 7

Les Corps conducteurs:
Frames of Reference[1]

I *Introduction*

IN 1970 Simon published with Skira in the series "Les Sentiers de la Création" a volume of prose, with accompanying illustrations generally consisting of reproductions of paintings, drawings, sculptures. This work was entitled *Orion aveugle* (*Blind Orion*), a title presumably chosen because of the role played in the prose by Poussin's painting of the same title, whose reproduction is also included. The text of the volume is the first, shorter version of what was to become *Les Corps conducteurs*, comprising the first eighty-seven pages of the novel as well as portions of its conclusion. The book is helpful in that it provides some of the visual material that will become a major element of the novel; but more importantly, it is prefaced by some considerations by Simon on his activity as a writer, and specifically on the present work. The chief importance that the text as such has acquired for him, as well as the development of this emphasis, are particularly underlined.[2] It is evident that he looks upon this direction as ultimately the more fruitful. He sees his work since *The Flanders Road* as an arduous liberation: "(...it takes time to get rid little by little of ingrained bad habits ...)."[3] *Orion aveugle*, the text, that is, seems to him now to lead somewhere else, to a complete novel whose path, he feels, may be different from those normally followed by the novelist, in that the beginning and the end will lose their importance in favor of the traveled road. He concludes by stating that this novel, "will not tell the exemplary story of some hero or heroine, but that quite different story of the singular adventure of a narrator who does not cease to search, warily discovering the world in and through writing."

Simon's shift towards this point of view was not drastic, as he himself admits, although anyone reading *Les Corps conducteurs,* for instance, after reading *The Palace,* could not fail to see it as such. We would situate the transition more particularly in *The Battle of Pharsalus,* whose third part, while it achieves the necessary concluding equilibrium, does so in a form anticipating that of *Les Corps conducteurs.* The present participle is no longer predominant, and sentences tend to be shorter; they are, on the surface, strictly objective descriptions of sense perceptions, largely visual. The vantage point of all previous novels, including two-thirds of *The Battle of Pharsalus,* a pervasive central consciousness, occupies now a peripheral position. There remains in *Les Corps conducteurs* a principal character engaged in the larger portion of the action, but his role is decisively secondary to that of the "writing," his action a correlative of the true plot; his several manifestations (as a sick man, a passenger on an airplane, a man resisting the end of an affair) remain the related expressions of a developing text and are linked by it rather than by any circumstantial evidence.

Les Corps conducteurs appeared in 1971. The title reflects the idea of conductance and that of direction. These "conductors" are the elements of the text, be it objects of description or aspects of the description per se, that effect the transition from one level of narration to another or one sequence to another; they are also the main sequences, several aspects of the same journey.

An initial reading of the novel gives the impression of discontinuity. Sequences are interposed by the text seemingly at random; none appears to conclude; none may definitely be seen as the continuation of any other. A man sits on a fire hydrant in a crowded street, pain radiating from the area of his liver and cold perspiration bathing his body; his eyes register his surroundings in great detail. The same man, presumably, sees a doctor about a liver ailment. We do not know whether the visit takes place before or after the scenes in the street. Another episode recounts the penetration deep into the jungle by an exploratory expedition; it takes place mostly in the sixteenth century but includes several times more recent direct recollections of a similar enterprise. High above the clouds an airplane is crossing the American continent, sometimes over jungles, over high mountain ranges, over cities at night. In it a passenger, perhaps the same man as before, grows progressively more uncomfortable, even feverish. He may be going to the congress of writers whose proceedings are followed in another narrative strand. The congress is held in Spanish in a Latin-American city, and its proceedings must be translated to the "foreigner" by an interpreter. Another sequence encompasses a shorter period of time, although it is pursued throughout the narrative: a man tries to reach a woman by telephone and does so eventually, only to hear her refuse to see him; later in the text (although not necessarily in time) a man (perhaps the same one) rises from a bed and sees his female companion standing in the doorway to the room, drinking a bowl of coffee. Other elements circulate through the fiction, independent of its main strands and yet closely echoing their principal elements; they consist mainly of careful descriptions of a variety of paintings, drawings, stamps and so on. Prominent among these are a study of Poussin's *Orion aveugle*, and the verbal transcription of several anatomical drawings of the human body.

It seems evident that in a composition such as *Les Corps conducteurs,* particular attention must be given to the elements that allow the transitions to take place from one sequence to another; likewise, the very nature of such transitions requires particular consideration. Also, although Simon has said that the situation at the end of the novel may well be quite similar to that at the beginning, it remains that the writing moves along certain paths, and that this movement should admit of definition. By examining the principal moments of several narrative sequences it should be possible to ascertain the direction of the text and perhaps map its most important stages.

Clearly, the fiction has assigned a major role to fixed representations, paintings, and so forth. This is not new in Simon. We recall the recurring portrait of the Conventionnel in *The Flanders Road,* the travel postcards of *Histoire,* the reproduced paintings and the bas-reliefs in *The Battle of Pharsalus.* In *Les Corps conducteurs* the radical autonomy of the text and its struggle against discontinuous action will assign an even greater function to designs already structured; these will stand out as portions of completion amid seeming fragmentation. It is through a consideration of these completed designs that the execution of the novel may reveal itself most distinctly.

II *Discontinuous Visions*

The first lines describe a row of plastic legs in a display window, half bent and feet up, identical. They remind the observer of a display of prosthetic limbs, a thought that introduces the description of a humorous picture representing an old professor and his students, happily preparing to dissect the body of an equally joyful, naked girl. A few short sentences unite both descriptions, emphasizing the laughter of the interns and the artificial smoothness of the legs. After this depiction of two designs, the central consciousness is introduced: "The doctor tells him to lower his trousers. At the end of the street he can see the avenue it crosses..."[4] (8). The display window encloses the row of legs much as the picture of the interns is itself contained in its frame; that is to say, they are both fully structured representations. By means of the vision of repeatedly severed legs and the drawing of the dissecting room, the idea of separation appears at the outset in one of its most important forms: representations of it, stated twice in two manners (window, picture of interns). Furthermore, this fragmentation is presented at the most unavoidable, basic level, that of the physical self, as an anticipation of death's final disjunction. Also, these images contain obvious humorous overtones, arising mainly from their incongruity (bodyless dancing legs, general hilarity in the gruesome task of dissecting).

The gathering of both visions in a few short sentences generates the appearance of the man. The idea of ridicule and the sight of naked legs naturally lead to the doctor's request; the latter's appearance confirms an undercurrent of bodily danger that will be confirmed a few lines later, as the personage suffers acute discomfort on the very street, and is forced to stop. The intrusion of the physician's request, and with it the entire sequence at the latter's office, is momentary, and is caused by the self-reinforcing suggestive power of both initial pictures. But the very sentence introducing the doctor contains the elements that allow a return to the original situation, in the street. In effect, the thought of lowered trousers suggests that of "crossing,"[5] and concurrently the image of the avenue "crossed" by the street. The activity of the text is itself here a "crossing over" from one sequence to another; this idea is reiterated in the next few lines where the distance to the "crossing with the avenue" is mentioned.

The entire descriptive complex functions as the metaphorical transformation and repetition of the same basic initial thoughts. The building at the corner of the avenue, for instance, is seen as "vertical and parallel lines, like organs" (9). We have an echo of the vertical row of legs, and an anticipation of the description of an anatomical drawing that is to follow (organs); the general connotations of the passage (fear of illness and death as the final "rending") is further maintained in that organs suggest church music and possibly a funeral service. This thought becomes more evident if we examine the entire passage: "The sparse leaves of the trees, of a green tending to ochre or even rust, papery and sickly, stir slightly in front of the grayish background of the building that rises at the corner of the street and the avenue in parallel vertical lines, like organs. In the opening of the narrow trench formed by the high façades one can see the white sky" (9). The implications are quite clear, particularly when we consider that the connotations of each word in a description are always eventually reinforcing. The "narrow trench" opening upon a "white sky" ("ciel" in French is both sky and heaven) is reminiscent of the grave, particularly since the whiteness of the sky is an indication of the sun's heat and the fever it exacerbates. As we shall see, whiteness is a frequent corollary of fever and death. As the display window with its row of legs reappears (introduced by the street's "verticality"), the presence of the sick man asserts itself, his fingers carefully feeling the area of his liver. The first anatomical description follows, a section of the abdomen where "one can see purple or bluish *organs*" (9) (italics mine).

As we have seen in the preceding chapters, the merest penetration below the surface of Simon's compact prose may reveal basic elements in the total composition. We have also found this to be true at all points in the several novels, although in the normal chronology of examination some particular attention was generally devoted to their opening passages. In the present instance, several major points of reference already chart a direction. The novel opens with a *picture* of fragmentation relative to the human body, an individual manifestation of the general movement towards discontinuity displayed by the novel as a whole and which the novel itself, as a *representation,* contains. This tendency is in its turn revealed at the middle level of action, in terms of the two important sequences initiated so far: the man in the street, ill and at the doctor's, apprehensive and humiliated. These two strongly related narrative strands both underline the fear of death, the ultimate separation, and, as implied by some aspects of the descriptions, that of castration, its equally distressing corollary: the description of the legs and that of the young girl on the dissecting table present the antagonism between eroticism and the idea of sectioning; as he lowers his trousers, the man notices his wilted member. Furthermore, the objects described illustrate the idea of a dispersion, either in fact (legs) or by implication (dissection). The anatomical drawing is a striking example of this; individual, internal organs are contained by the outer envelope: "... the abdominal wall has been cut out, as if a lid had been withdrawn" (9). Even the shape of the section is described in terms of a completed form: "about the shape of the soundbox of a guitar" (9). The area of discomfort, by contrast, is seen as shapeless: "Where his fingers press there is a mass with soft contours, brick-red, like a sack" (9).

The main sequences to be introduced are the jungle expedition and the airplane journey. The sick man, looking at the wall of a building, notices a religious formula painted thereon: "*DIOS ES AMOR*" (13). He notes the irregularity of the lettering, "the slight sinuosities of the path followed by the paint when it slipped" (14). Above the letters, the arms of a cross, "also drip rivulets of white blood" (14). At this point the text moves to the description of a stamp wherein a bald, bearded man stands on a beach, one hand holding aloft a crucifix to which he points with the other. Soldiers and Indians surround him. Simon[6] himself, as an example of the activity of the text, has pointed out how "cross" and "crucifix" create here the transition from one narrative strand to another .Other aspects of this transition to the jungle sequence also deserve notice: Once more we note that the transfer is effected between two described designs, the second one becoming the initial moment in one of the most important continuities of the book. Further, as before, there are evident anticipations of its later stages: "slight sinuosities of the path" suggests the river followed by the expedition; "rivulets of white blood," while also pointing to the shape and setting of the journey (rivulets = rivers), likewise refers to its circumstances: the blood shed by white men. Here also white is the color of death. The emergence of the airplane sequence follows a similar pattern and is controlled by the same motif. The cross held in the old warrior's "steel gloved hand" (15) is surrounded by diverging rays, "like a sun in a sky the color of absinthe" (15). The conjunction of "steel," "cross," "sun," and "sky" calls forth "The cross-shaped shadow of the airplane" (15). Here also the transition proceeds from one design to another: the airplane is seen in terms of the shadow it draws on the forest. Its journey will closely parallel that of the expedition in the jungle, as anticipated by the relationship already established upon the initial emergence of both sequences.

Inserted between two anatomical descriptions, the narrative strand recounting the severance of the sexual relationship already displays the kinship of this event to the fear of illness and death. The woman and child now introduced are the first form of the final sequence involving the couple in the anguish of their separation. It appears in the context of the street scenes already presented at the very beginning. From the anatomical drawing we return to the sick man sitting on a fire hydrant. In his mouth an unlit cigarette is "quavering with slight up and down movements communicated to it by the trembling of the lips" (16). The toy pulled by a child is animated by an analogous movement: "A system of simple mechanical relays drives the arms of the rabbit ... the arms rise and fall in turn ..." (16–17). As we see, the description of the motion elicits the rabbit's appearance, not the man's consciousness or his field of vision. Again, reality is subject to the decisions of language. Similarly, the shift from the woman and child to the continuing anatomical design is a purely verbal occurrence: the tinkling of the toy introduces a description of the body by means of the word *grêle*, or *intestin grêle* (small intestine) (p. 17), an approximation of *grelot* ("small bell").

The last sequence to be introduced, one of major importance, is the writers' congress. The images that precede it prepare for its emergence. In the vision of a condor, in flight, and then tearing at a rotting mass of flesh, is contained the principal narrative strands so far introduced: it suggests the forest whose numerous birds are frequently mentioned and described in the context of the expedition; the condor's flying and appearance—"its feathers have the consistency and the blue glints of steel" (32) —recall the airplane; he is pulling at "Rubbery ribbons of intestine or of dead flesh" (33), bringing to mind the anatomical descriptions as well as the fear of illness and death. As previously, the introduction of a new sequence is preceded by a convergence of former ones. The depiction of a building palisade that now follows anticipates the implications of the congress sequence, as it lingers for a moment on the discolored, tattered remnants of bills pasted on it: the condor's feed: "the ribbons of stinking meat" brings in the "tatters of posters" (33). The ensuing lines stress the difficulty of completing the written fragments of the posters, although such a reconstruction is possible: "The texts of the torn posters seem however (unless it is simply a matter of coincidence, or the result of a particular turn of mind of the decipherer) to have been of a political nature" (33). The central character is introduced as a "decipherer," possibly an unreliable one. This announces the situation of the writer in the congress and also points to the necessary participation and activity of the novel's reader. Incomplete words are given as *examples* of the type of reconstruction involved in understanding the fragments; the emphasis falls on the reconstruction itself, rather than on its object, a familiar situation in Simon whereby once more our attention is drawn away from the represented and to the text: "No word is entirely visible. There remain only a few enigmatic fragments ... allowing for one or several interpretations (or reconstructions) such as, for example, ABOR (lABOR, or ABORto, or ABORrecer?) ..." (33). The first scene of the writers' congress is elicited by the assumed political tenor of these announcements. Again underlined are the difficulties of understanding the speech in progress, the effort to translate the few terms familiar to the foreign participant intruding on the general continuity of the language. The "decipherer" is thus introduced here also, and the entire episode becomes an amplification of the previous moment. A tentative reconstruction is here likewise suggested: the address seems to consist of general considerations of a social or political nature, with frequent references to "nouns with a slightly timeworn air, like the colors of the posters" (34).

The sequence, introduced by means of a design, as were the previous ones, continues in its first stage to develop as a fixed representation, pursuing thus an established pattern. The description stresses its most obviously static elements: the first images are those of the coat of arms of the host country.[7] The initial personage in this sequence, the president of the assembly, is introduced by a metaphor that recalls the appearance of another important character, the "old warrior": trumpets, sounded by two angels on the coat of arms, "spread in divergent rays, like those of a sun or the spokes of a fan" (35). Rising above the lectern, "the bust of the president appears" (35). The account of the scene continues to detail stationary forms: furniture, objects, even the paper provided for the delegates take precedence. As the text focuses on the capitalized Latin inscription that heads these blank sheets, we return to the street scene where similar inscriptions had provided the representational bridge to the congress sequence.

III   Elusive Fixity

The first pages (to p. 35) have introduced those narrative strands which the novel will henceforth pursue: (1) the sick man in the street; (2) the visit to the doctor; (3) the expedition in the jungle; (4) the airplane journey; (5) the woman and child, a first aspect of the "parting lovers" sequence developed principally in the last third of the book; (6) the writers' congress. They have all originated from the description of a static design, a composition that was already structured or which the text organized in some pattern (e.g., the congress). Except for the jungle expedition, we may assume that the same character is the center of observation in all cases. Although this does not as yet appear to be a factor of particular importance, the reader's desire to create such a continuity is itself significant, validated by the text, as it were, since it explicitly points to the desire for completion as characteristic of the observer. It is this thirst for completion that calls for fixed representations as the starting points of the main narrative sequences. It is also because of this preference for structured fixity that the majority of transitions are effected through that very medium. The transforming image in sequences 1 to 4 is that of the cross, where the narrative chooses this very design to achieve the "crossing over." Sequence 5 belongs as yet properly to sequence 1, the street scene; not yet a major narrative line, it does not warrant the mobilization of the main transfer mechanism. The congress sequence, by its very nature as the purported examination of the problems of writing, the significance of creating fictions and of interpreting words, is introduced through a comment on this same question of semantic interpretation. The designs that are used to support the transition are those proper to the character of the inquiry; they are words, and these words are presented as *drawings,* in capital letters. We have here not specifically a crossing over, but a translation. As pointed out above, the first moment of all of these narrative strands is either a fixed image, or, as in the case of the writers' congress again, an active scene described in terms of its fixity: surroundings, furniture, pictures, static designs. The sequences are thus initiated from a position of strength, contained by clearly definable frames. Subsequently, this coherence will be undermined from all sides toward a final dispersion.

Although all six narrative strands circulate through the fiction with comparable frequency, the airplane journey, the jungle expedition and the writers' congress offer the most visibly structured points of departure from which to follow a general development. The airplane is introduced through a transition from the first image of the jungle sequence; the latter is itself directly linked at the outset with the writers' congress by means of the paintings, coat of arms, and other pictorial references to the origins of the host country. The initial account of the writers' assembly extends over approximately ten pages, interrupted by a segment of the street scene and a few lines on the view from the airplane. The street scene ends on a vision of the crowd,

"multitudes condemned to turn endlessly, to retrace their steps
and set out again inside an enclosed space deprived of sky" (37).
This thought of endless enclosed repetition calls forth the president's speech and the undertaking of the congress given as an
outline, an overview similar to that of the street which introduced it. The assembly's organized schedule is thus already
placed under the pall of inconclusive circularity. The foreign
writer refuses at first his journalist companion's offer to translate
for him the president's words. This allows another objective
description to take the place of the speech, that is to say, the
penetration of extraneous language into the fiction's own prose
is postponed for a moment, holding at bay the disruption of its
flow. The text may then proceed to considerations on the body
of delegates, deriving unifying generalities from their appearance and demeanor.

Such observations, about the physical and psychological
characteristics common to most of the representatives, lead quite
naturally to their common ancestry, composed of adventurers
and explorers, and thus to another stage of the expedition's
progress. The terrain now imposes a division of forces; the
leader is obliged to leave half of his vessels and sailors behind.
Indians appear, fearful, awed perhaps by the size of the boats
and the strange appearance of the men. The view from the airplane which now issues forth becomes a correlative of the
Indians' terror and wonder: "The dorsal fin of the leviathan
slowly pivots, drifting to one side of the airplane, offering its
glistening slopes one after the other, terrifying in its terrifying
solitude, the terrifying silence of thousands of years" (40). The
mention of awesome size links the view from the plane with
the preceding description of the ships' arrival, from the Indians'
supposed point of view; the "glistening" of the "slopes" links it
with the account of disembarkation that follows, the reference
becoming more specific and centering on the presence of the
leader "whose long beard overflows on his breastplate in the
shape of a ship's prow gleaming in the sun" (40).

The penetration of the airplane sequence into that of the
expedition restates the idea of scission already present in the
first division of the expeditionary contingent; it separates one
single event, the landing, into two portions. The details of the

description are altered by this intrusion. The leader, first seen as a general, becomes in the second part "the old man" (40); this slight shift towards a deterioration of the main element of cohesion in the foreign troops is countered by the transformation of this scene into its more structured counterpart, a commemorative stamp (strongly resembling the one that opened the entire sequence). In this scene, as a reflection of newly recaptured unity, the faces of the soldiers are described as "bold, firmly resolute" (41). The few sentences pertaining to the airplane's flight, although contributing, by their intrusion in its midst, to the incipient fragmentation of the expedition sequence, represent at the verbal level an instance of the novel's more intrinsic structure. The image of the mountain crest is an echo of the preceding passage, while it merges with the one that follows, thus maintaining an unbroken metaphorical movement. Hence, the increasing dispersion which characterizes the narrative lines is restrained by the underlying cohesiveness of the text. Their mounting fragmentation undermines the initial independence of these lines and allows language to assert its predominance as they weaken. Moving to the next level of composition, the jungle expedition would then appear, at this point, as a prolonged interruption of the ongoing writers' congress, while containing elements common to both itself and the congress. Such is in fact the case: the counterpart of the commemorative stamp is the painting of a battle that fills the wall behind the president; it may be seen as a later moment in the evolution of both groups, white men and Indians, or half-breeds, now in open conflict.

	Stamp:		*Painting:*
I	1. old man with white beard	II	1. leader with ebony beard
	2. soldiers		2. horsemen
	3. cross surrounded by rays		3. mission belfry
	4. Indians with naked bodies		4. men with wide straw hats and drooping moustaches

The president is seen against the background of the painting, his bust surrounded by the fighting. This image anticipates

the final disruption of the congress, whose inconclusive adjourn-
ment arises from an unresolved political situation: various delegates consider that the present discussions do not address themselves to the immediate problem of repression and poverty in the
land. The present situation is a counterpart of the painted combat. At the textual level, the introduction of Spanish sentences
constitutes an evident intrusion into the unified course of the
language. As yet, the break is somewhat mitigated by the fact
that several sentences are translated at once, the French and
the Spanish separated by a short descriptive passage that further
allays the disruption, so that the disturbance of the page is slight.

Henceforth, the formal schedule of the congress gradually
deteriorates; political-minded delegates interrupt the proceedings
to demand consideration for social issues. The speeches are
translated for the foreign participant; the original Spanish,
slashed into small segments for comprehension, penetrates the
running text, rending the fabric of the novel's language. A
temporary unity is achieved by the overwhelming thundering
applause that greets one of the partisan statements, the description of this event then allowing the prose to proceed untrammeled. In view of the impasse, the president, furious, terminates
the session at this point.

The jungle expedition undergoes a similar temporary restructuring in a passage immediately preceding the closing of the
writers' meeting. The medium employed is a photograph, a choice
that remains in strict agreement with the predominance given to
pictorial representations in the development of this sequence.
The quality of the reproduction is such that the details are lost
in a "sooty scrawl dotted with light patches or scratched with
lines in every direction, like a child's scribble, the surface
of the page crossed out as if by an angry hand" (102). The
imperfections of design, the scratches and blots, are to the photograph what the applause, as sound, was to the speeches of the
convention. This parallelism is clearly implied by the language
of the above quotation, the emotion it denotes reminiscent of
that pervading the assembly. The relationship becomes even
clearer as the expeditionary troop is described "moving through
a frantic hailstorm of streaks..." (102), the lines explicitly
compared to sound.

We have reached, midway through the novel, a moment where new possibilities of cohesiveness are tentatively offered, as in a last gathering of strength before the ultimate dissolution. Once more, the airplane sequence intrudes into that of the expedition. The machine's appearance is prepared through an emphasis on light and refraction imagery, recalling that last convergence of the two narrative lines. Light is reflected on the leaves; occasionally "the sun lights up blinding stars ... among which a bright yellow spot slackly drifts, fluttering incoherently ... like a light piece of paper" (108). The butterfly, subsequently described in great detail, is a clear correlative of the aircraft. More significant still, it introduces, by means of the insect's accurate depiction that follows, a specific aspect of the plane journey: the passenger is passing the time by reading a magazine devoted to various aspects of the jungle, and accompanied by numerous illustrations, particularly of birds and butterflies. The actual "crossover" of the jungle and airplane sequence takes place a few lines later as the jet flies over the expedition: "At one point, however, as it shifts course slightly, the sun glimmers on the fuselage, the time of a flash" (110). Although it is not explicitly mentioned, the image of a shining cross is obvious. From now on, the airplane sequence will remain almost invariably linked to that of the jungle. Material from the publications that the passenger examines will provide embellishment and pictorial accuracy to the action below. Still, the expedition's march toward ultimate disintegration will continue unabated, so that a mutual undermining will develop, whereby the passenger's fatigue seems to be a reflection of the explorers' ordeal; similarly, the information provided by the magazine has the effect of inflicting further hardships on the men in the forest (poisons, insects, etc.).

The column now begins to stretch out to dangerous limits; wounded laggards must be protected. But there are as yet no actual losses of men. The leader is described in terms of power, vigor, and persistence, as he was at first. The pages on the convention that follow depict a moment when the focus of cohesion also seems to gather for a final attempt. The delegates, now as a study group, look composed and reasonable. Soon, however, the mutually undermining effect of these two sequences also begins to be felt. The resumption of the speeches is preceded by a description of a "laughing bird" (126) and its repeated guffaws. The translation once more severs the text; the expeditionary column begins to develop wider gaps.

Until the end, the process of mutual erosion heretofore examined in the context of these three narrative lines (airplane, jungle, congress), and which remains operative also for the other three (street, woman, doctor), will accelerate their fragmentation. The shifts will be more frequent as imagery charged with previously accumulated connotations transforms each segment into the close correlative of all the others. The incidents of the jungle expedition are gradually displaced by material from the magazines read on the airplane, even including portions of their written text whose less disciplined style is easily recognizable. The writers' congress degenerates into a series of quarrels marked by rudeness. The airplane journey, having now in a sense taken over most of the elements of the jungle adventure, no longer affords sight of the ground. Instead, the view appears circumscribed by the porthole, one half filled with clouds, the other with sky, an image of division.

IV *The Unified Design*

Thus, gradual dispersion of incidental content, rather than undermining the structure of the narrative, allows its underpinning, language, metaphor, and image, to attain the full compositional significance wherein the novel achieves its cohesiveness. In the broader scheme also, pictorial representations fulfill a crucial role: they gauge the progress of the dispersion while providing moments of possible reorganization; they are the point of departure of all the main sequences as well as their conclusion; and they prove peculiarly fertile ground for the text to develop the internal correspondences that constitute its basic pattern.

The image of the cross, which in the early part of the novel was the basic transitional element, is quickly joined by that of brilliance, also the common element of several sequences (jungle and plane for instance), and then replaced by it. The role of light and refraction is particularly apt when used as a metaphor of transfer to a pictorial representation where masses of darkness and clarity are essential components. Such is the manner in which appear, initially, the erotically charged sequences, which give rise to a countermovement toward the increasing fragmentation of the main episodes.

As we saw earlier, the illness of the central character was closely associated with the idea of surgical severance and, given the sexual connotations of his vision, with that of impotence or castration. His separation from his mistress is restated, as it were, with each one of his conversations with her over the telephone; when he does reach her, she denies his requests, regardless of his entreaties. In the last stage of this sequence, he is separated from her by the length of the room, his desire focused on the very act of seeing her half-naked form, his eyes trying to fill the distance between them. Light, the sun shining upon the scene, underlines this distance as it marks its duration. Light also introduces a movement towards possible union; images of coitus are described in an attempt to create moments of coherence; the detail of the scenes as well as the completion of their form appear as bulwarks against the otherwise increasing discontinuity, one outcome of which is the final distance between the main character and his mistress.

The depiction of constellations, soon to become one of cosmic coupling, first appears directly linked to the woman-child couple. Dropped from the child's hand, the rope that pulled his toy, "winds [*serpente*] on the sidewalk in slack curves" (29). This design on the ground, in a shift parallel to that linking the jungle and airplane sequences, turns into a design in the firmament: "The serpent is an equatorial constellation..." (29). The image is immediately followed by a segment of the airplane sequence. These lines prepare a later scene that will in its turn develop into two narrative lines of lesser textual elaboration but of some structural consequence. It is introduced by the progression: telephone—elderly woman walking across the hotel lobby—telephone—airplane—stars (invisible) = constellations (55–59). The slow and difficult progress of the old woman towards the sunny street anticipates one of the lines to emerge from the passage: blind Orion walking towards the rising sun. The invisibility of the stars from the airplane clearly points to the link between the two narrative lines (airplane, constellations) as a matter of words, rather than sense impressions. Whether the stars are visible or not, the presence of the word itself on the page is sufficient to elicit the passage that follows on the disposition of various astral groups. In effect, the transition is not to the night sky but to its allegorical map. The second strand of narration evolving from this scene originates in the implications of the telephone call and becomes a series of images of coitus.

From this point on, these two lines of narrative, charged with the imagery of light conferred upon them by their initial condition, will undergo a parallel development to create temporary moments of cohesiveness in the text by means of ramifications of imagery of light (or darkness) and vision (or blindness). They will constitute the representational correlative of two central sequences: the erotic descriptions will correspond to the scene of the man and woman parting, those of Poussin's Orion to the sick man's painful progress through the street.

Astral bodies seen in terms of the ancient figures they were thought to suggest become effective pictorial instances of resolved discontinuity. The shapes "Etched with a burin" (55) encompass geometric patterns formed by the constellations. As the description of this astronomical map continues, it endows its forms with the pulsation of life and prefigures a titanic coitus. "The milky light" (56) of night introduces an embracing couple on a bed whose shapes are seen in terms of their isolated darker regions, a counterpart of the stars contained by the mythical bodies. The two forms are then considered in their total mass, undivided and situated in the heavens. As the intertwined couple reassume the immense proportions of astral configurations, their "bodies . . . clutching one another" (57) summon the image of the giant Orion, and the constellation of the same name. After a return to the vast copulating bodies, the image of the blind giant takes its final form in the painting by Poussin. It is seen as a whole, with emphasis on the figure's hugeness. Both series of images have evolved in the same direction, from circumscribed plurality, through an intermediary stage where masses predominate, to a final accent on unity.

In the next stage, these two sets of images have already had

their newfound wholeness undermined by the irresistible drift
toward discontinuity of the entire narrative. The same episodes
that introduced them before continue to do so: old woman
walking—woman and child—airplane and light. The coupled
bodies display their internal organs through *transparent* light
openings. In Poussin's painting the giant's body is seen surrounded by trees and *clotted* masses of clouds. In both cases
the original "wholes" suffer an initial parceling. The subsequent
renditions of each scene display an increasing loss of unity; the
couple is no longer joined, and Orion's form now seems to be
diminished, sinking into the scenery: "He appears . . . like a bas-
relief figure, stuck to the décor . . ." (77). As we noted, around
the middle of the novel a new effort to find unity manifests
itself. The man finally reaches his mistress by telephone, amid
a welter of placards and graffiti whose capitals overwhelm on
the page the normally written text. The incident takes place
in a subway station, as the crashing sound of the trains and the
moral and religious exhortations screaming out of the walls
drown the halting telephone conversation. We encounter the
same type of rearguard, temporary coherence presented by the
applause in the congress sequence and the bad photograph in
the jungle sequence. The notices on the wall provide an ironic
commentary to this less than satisfactory reunion of the man
and the woman, a reunion situated by the man at the level of
life or death: "JESUS VIDA ETERNA . . . TU QUE BUSCAS EN LAS
TINIEBLAS . . . IT IS NEVER TOO LATE" (93). ("Jesus Eternal Life,
You who seek in the dark . . ."). The most frequent statements
refer indirectly to his plight. They are, in fact, its capitalized
condensation, and in this manner, provide a species of temporary
circumscription of its elements, including the telephone call.
Orion's description also suggests a renewed effort toward comprehension in that it underlines the very activity of containing:
"fine lines etched with a burin, following the bulge of the
muscles, the contours of the limbs, more or less dense, criss-
crossing in the darker parts, like the meshes of a net" (112); it is
accompanied by general mention of constellations in terms of
their broader masses. The erotic scenes find temporary cohesion
in a picture of copulation that anticipates the description of a
Picasso drawing of a similar scene in later pages. Although the

coitus is not seen in a moment of complete union, this eventuality
is imminent and thus represents an instance of lesser dispersion.

The actual rendering of the drawing[8] already indicates a
definite relapse into disunity. It is elicited by a segment of the
airplane sequence; the passenger is reading a magazine article
on the jungle, where the trees seem "the springing up of the
trunks as columns smoother than marble" (131). Fatigue draws
"small burning cracks" (131) on his features. These images,
containing connotations of light and suggesting deeply etched
lines, call forth the furrowed face of the old king in the erotic
picture, watching the young lovers with a desolate eye. The
latter are seen as "fragments of jigsaw puzzles with sinuous
edges" (133); the entire description is interrupted by returns to
the airplane sequence, and the expression of the passenger's
discomfort establishes a clear correspondence between himself
and the onlooking king; his eyes feel as if "intangible grains of
sand tore the cornea" (132). The presence of pain and the
anguish of death have been closely linked with eroticism from
the outset, becoming more explicit as the images that contained
them tended toward disunity. These connotations have also been
related to imagery of light, as when the lovers' internal organs
appeared through transparent sections of their skin, or in the
present case by means of the torn cornea and fever. They are
evident projections of the main character's own dread, while his
fatigue (or illness in the street sequence) is related to his
separation from his mistress and his fear of dying.

Two subsequent passages, corresponding to the final sequence
where the couple are divided by the length of a room and eyes
establish their only contact, offer pictorial expressions of these
very circumstances. The sick man examines the window of a sex
boutique, where women display their genitals on the covers of
magazines in a variety of lubricious poses, next to similar,
though less provocative, photographs of naked men. Another
display window, an optician's, offers a magnified section of the
eye. The men and women are separately photographed and separately displayed; sexual union is reduced to voyeurism, has
become a function of sight. To underline this, the eye, also
isolated, is displayed in the next shop.

The first segment of the episode where the two lovers part

follows a passage on the writers' conference, where the principal element is the newspaper examined by one of the delegates. Among the most important components to effect the transition from one sequence to the other are: (1) the newspaper page which seems "a checkerboard of small rectangles" (152); (2) an accumulation of capitalized titles of films, reminiscent of the posted announcements that surrounded the telephone conversation; (3) examples of the pictures adjoining the cinema advertisements: "a man and a woman embracing, the Chinese-shadow silhouette of a woman in a transparent shift" (152). The role of item 2 as a transferring agent arises from the previous proximity of capitalized statements to the first attempt to bridge the distance between the lovers, through a telephone call. Element 1 is repeatedly echoed by the details of the parting scene: ". . . he sees floating . . . the rectangle of the door framing the silhouette"; "the tiling of the kitchen"; "another door in whose rectangle (distorted by perspective into a trapezoid)"; "a window"; "One distinguishes clearly the bricks of the chimney" (153). Element 3 has become the half-naked woman whose presence pervades the scene.

The sequence leads to the woman's refusal of her companion's requests, and an increase in the distance between them. The approach of these two inevitabilities may be gauged by the development of the imagery that has from the beginning accompanied all sexual connotations, and which in this instance becomes a pattern of sunlight on the floor. As the man awakens to find the woman gone from his side, the sun has not yet risen. The next scene shows the orange glow of dawn lighting the white wall of the bathroom; in subsequent segments the light will penetrate into the room, drawing the shape of the window on the floor. The progress and steady alteration of this rectangle of light will mark the man's gradual realization of the hopelessness of his entreaties, the inevitability of the rupture. In the last moments, the patch of sunlight breaks up, becomes two thin lines, two threads of incandescence, and disappears: "Soon nothing on the wall or on the tiling recalls its place" (224). Orion's image will similarly disappear, together with the light of its stars. At the moment when the stars fade, the final vision of the giant's form merges the constellation with Poussin's painting. The night was not sufficient for him to reach his goal: "Every-thing indicates that he shall never reach his goal" (222).

While the reader, as a matter of course, has assumed the protagonist of each sequence to be the same man, one of the clearest confirmations of this intuition arises from the internal evidence that links the various narrative sequences to one another and unfolds their parallel structure. Their episodes become alternative versions of the same basic movement towards disjunction, while the visions of each experience are but aspects of the same mind. This condition becomes especially clear when considering the role played by the figure of Orion, and that of the old king in the cubist drawing; in each instance the text indicates the protagonist's identification with both personages. The description of Picasso's drawing emphasizes the contrast between the youthfulness of the lovers and the king's age, plainly suggesting the latter's impotence as the reason for his despair. Since all the erotic descriptions in the novel are introduced by the imagery of light, the central character's further likening to blind Orion clearly points also either to his impotence or to his fear of it: in this case, not seeing is the same as being sexually inadequate. Sexual union becomes then the epitome of the narrator's search for completion; impotency (castration) and death are comparable in that they both represent a severance. The man's illness is both the origin and the result of his inade-quacy, as well as of his fear of death, the irreversible disjunction.

Entering his hotel room, the sick man falls on the rug, whose secondary pattern is now visible, close to his eyes: "Seen thus, from up close, the contours of the flowers, of the leaves, the veins, following the weave, follow a steplike pattern" (226); looking carefully, one may even see "the gray and parallel lines of the threadbare weave" (226). The divisions of the narrative, as well as their individual discontinuities, were merely a surface phenomenon. Beneath this surface, the text has composed a pattern where the disposition toward fragmentation is not only contained, but transformed into an element of cohesion.

CHAPTER 8

Triptyque: *Multiple Montages*

I *Introduction*

IN *Triptyque*, Simon pursues his research into language as an instrument of autonomous, self-referential creation. To this end, traditional novelistic features have been further stripped away, allowing exceptional freedom to the flow of the text and a wider range to its invention. The resolve to expunge the central consciousness from narrative, for instance, finds here its fullest expression. One impersonal observer remained even in the third part of *The Battle of Pharsalus*, and we could assign the activities of five of the six main sequences in *Les Corps conducteurs* to the same character. *Triptyque* permits no such focus. Although we are explicitly told of the strong similarity between two individuals in separate sequences, this is attributed to the probable identity of the actor in the two films which are part of these episodes. The situation is the reverse of that in *Les Corps conducteurs*: instead of various visions comparable through their singular source, we witness one central vision subsuming at least two separate roles. That is to say, through emphasis on the idea of representation (the same *actor* in two *films*), the text points to itself as the inventor and the equalizer of all individual characteristics. The supremacy of the writing as such is apparent in both novels, although more decisively so in *Triptyque*, where it creates relationships ex nihilo and evolves its substance through the very blatancy of this act.

With *Triptyque*, Simon's predilection for using visual elements as the starting point of his fiction has also advanced further. The idea of words as pictures and sounds prevailed in *The Battle of Pharsalus*; in *Les Corps conducteurs*, while the same concern remained (for Simon prefers adaptation to replacement), the more strictly pictorial qualities of paintings and drawings took precedence. In *Triptyque*, the use of film offers a medium

167

that includes both language and image, while retaining an important function for them individually. Similarly, although his fiction deals increasingly with the concept of action as multi-faceted representation, Simon's attention to the themes of death (or violence) and eroticism has not lagged: they constitute the center of circumstance in the narrative's three parallel "stories." In effect, each of the three main sequences in the fiction develops around a sexual encounter which is either the consequence or the cause of some disastrous event.

The novel is divided into three parts, of which the middle one is significantly longer, each one comprising interthreaded segments of three lines of action, situated in three different French localities: a hamlet in a valley, a resort in the South, and a northern industrial city. A reconstruction of the events poses two types of difficulties: the sequences of the hamlet and the industrial center undergo drastic temporal displacements in Part III, and the incidents elucidating the resort sequence must be conjectured from a limited number of details. As with Simon's other novels, the true plot of *Triptyque* is that of its structure, wherein the stories find their place as individual elements. Nevertheless, it is useful for purposes of clarification and background to delineate the principal circumstantial sequences, and to establish thereby an adequate referential basis.

The main episode in the hamlet concerns the sexual encounter in a barn of a young servant with a farm worker, and its consequences. The woman leaves her small daughter in the care of two young boys who in turn leave the child with two older girls. She then walks to the barn where her lover has arrived on his motorcycle. The lovemaking proceeds through three stages: coitus, fellatio, and cunnilingus. In the meantime the little girl has been abandoned by her two older companions. We see the servant in tears later, in the farm where she is employed, and we surmise from the activity on the riverbank that her daughter has fallen in and drowned.

In the northern city a wedding procession is stopped for some moments at a railroad crossing; across the street a barmaid stands in front of a neighborhood café. Later in the day the groom and his male wedding companions arrive at the same café for drinks. The barmaid and the groom, who seem to know one another, slip out of the café to the back alley where they make love in the rain, standing against a brick wall. This embrace also progresses through three stages: (1) preliminary caresses and first penetration; (2) second penetration (necessitated by the groom's drunkenness and the awkwardness of the position) and completion; (3) separation and vomiting by the groom, followed by the young woman's attempt to clean the vomit from the man's suit and her own legs. The groom then rejects the barmaid, who tries to detain him; in a struggle around his car he loses his keys and decides to walk home. A man, who had been in the café throughout and who seems to be familiar with the barmaid, follows him on a motorcycle. Later that night, the groom, battered and still drunk, returns to his hotel room and falls asleep naked on the bed. His bride undresses and remains standing in front of a mirror.

In the seaside resort a naked woman lies on a bed in a hotel room, her position suggesting recently ended lovemaking. A man is dressing in front of the mirror. Their conversation implies that the woman's favors have been granted in exchange for the man's possible intercession with the authorities, regarding difficulties in which her son finds himself.[1] The man signifies that money must change hands. The headline of a half-crumpled newspaper on the floor mentions high school boys involved in drug trafficking; this, together with other details, intimates that such is precisely the situation in which the woman's son is involved. The man suggests to her that she solicit the help of someone she has been seen with, apparently a rich Anglo-Saxon named Brown. It is this man who presumably is talking to her later; she is still in bed in the same position. Brown is then seen selling some jewelry and giving the money to a dubious-looking character in a bar, in exchange for some small packets of powder. He informs the woman (Corinne) that her son will be freed that evening. He then goes to his own room where he completes a jigsaw puzzle showing the hamlet, the river, and so forth. After placing the last piece, he brushes it off the table in disgust. The film ends on this scene, and the novel concludes as the spectators in the cinema, in the northern industrial city, put on their coats and walk out into the rainy, deserted streets. Corinne's form on the bed is described in three stages also: one with the first man, Lambert; one with Brown before his transaction; and the last one with him after the transaction. The lovemaking itself is not part of this sequence, although we may easily surmise it. The structure of this episode is somewhat different from that of the other two, for the catastrophe is averted at the last minute, although not because of Corinne's surrender to Lambert, but rather because of the money paid. In the previous episodes, however, the lovemaking was responsible for the death of the little girl, in one case, and the marriage's inauspicious beginnings in the other. In all three instances, the scenes of explicit or potential disaster are absent, while the sexual encounters or their aftermaths are given in detail.

Together with these main story lines, other secondary scenes appear as accompanying developments that serve to anticipate, echo, and reinforce the central action. Apart from general descriptions of the three localities involved, there are seven attendant series of some importance: (1) an old woman going to feed some rabbits with a battered baby carriage full of grass; she kills one (the rabbit thereafter appears on the farm kitchen table, next to a postcard); (2) a boy doing a geometry problem and looking at a segment of film; (3) a boy herding some cows; (4) two boys swimming, fishing, looking at several segments of film, and spying on the couple in the barn; (5) a clown's act in a circus; (6) various descriptions of the showing of some films and the accidents of the presentation (the films slip, catch, and burn); (7) the description of some circus and movie posters. The first four of these secondary developments take place in the valley and may be seen as part of the barn sequence. The description of posters also originates here, and so does that of the clown's act. This fragmentation accurately reflects the general organization of the novel, growing like a mosaic, or like the village-scene puzzle which is dispersed at the end. On the other hand, these scenes, as we shall see, also function as metaphorical counterparts of the main action in three modes, themselves appearing as reflections of one another.

II *The Script*

Simon's choice of cinematic technique as an important medium is already apparent in the first pages of *Triptyque*. From the details of a color postcard of a Mediterranean resort, the field of vision widens in a backward zoom, to include the table where it lies, the kitchen, the farm, the hamlet, and the valley. As this "traveling" begins, the imperfections of the photograph are underlined, first as an overdramatization of color—"a sky too blue on the shore of a too blue sea."[2] (7)—then as a carelessness in design—"The inking of the different colors does not coincide exactly with the contours of each object..." (7). While our attention is drawn to the unsatisfactory character of this particular representation, the text attempts to provide a more adequate picture in the backward movement towards an overview of the valley, to correspond with the overview of the resort offered by the postcard. But having reached the most general angle of vision, new problems of focusing appear, which reveal the incompleteness of this perspective also: "From the barn one can see the steeple. From the foot of the cascade one can also see the steeple but not the barn. From the top of the cascade one can see both the steeple and the roof of the barn" (9). The moving camera, although it improves on the quality of colored, fixed images, presents problems of its own.

One of the first tasks of the text will be to try to find the correct focus and the right point of view with which to proceed. At the end, with the dispersion of the puzzle, other noises have begun to cover the sound of the film while the spectators get up and leave into the night, one representation, the text, overtaking the other. The conclusion of the narrative is thus an exact counterpart to its beginning, and both point to the central organizational principle of the novel as the unsuccessful search for an adequate representational mode (postcards, posters, puzzle, film, etc.), rendered in terms of a successful, all-encompassing one: the writing. The puzzle was as unsatisfactory as the postcard, and the movie itself was but one part of a great whole. The solutions offered by film throughout the novel will be only temporary, as were those offered by the paintings and drawings of *Les Corps conducteurs*, and always partial.

Although Brown discards the puzzle at the end, while his own action is effectively canceled by the film's concluding, the picture he created out of the jigsaw pieces offers a useful analogy to the manner in which the prose of *Triptyque* functions at its most immediate level, as well as an insight into some aspects of the novel's total structure. Here, perhaps more than ever, a view of the entire work is the indispensable preparation toward any understanding of its detail. In this sense, one could conceive of the narrative's progress as a mosaic that reconstitutes itself without the guidance of the completed picture. The components of the mosaic consist as much of individual portions of action as they do of varieties of representational modes. That is to say, the particular segments of story are contiguous to one another as much in terms of what they show (coitus, clown's act, café scene), as they are in terms of how these are shown (film, poster, straight narrative). To pursue the analogy with a puzzle or a mosaic, it is in the nature of such designs that from each individual piece radiate new possibilities of linkage, related to its shape, perhaps, or its principal colors, or its own particular portion of the picture. This manner of linking apparently disparate segments of prose was already an important element in the structure of *The Battle of Pharsalus;* it became more so in *Les Corps conducteurs,* and reaches its full realization with the present novel. We are therefore not dealing with something new in Simon, rather with the most decisive manifestation to date of a familiar concern.

The transitions, or links, between divers elements of the narrative, are effected in a variety of manners, among which the most frequent may be termed "rhyming."[3] It includes all species of resemblances between words, actions or images. We need but read a few pages to encounter numerous instances of these links. The text itself "teaches" the reader to notice the various bonds, moving away from obvious connections to more subtle ones; it effects thus its own liberation from the initial impositions of such broad concepts as point of view or perspective: "If one stares at the umbels, the steeple afar appears as a blurred gray rectangle, stretched upwards, surmounted by a purplish triangle, also blurred. At certain times, the sun glimmers on one or the other of the edges of rusty zinc. The stalks of the umbels are covered with a fine white down which in the backlighting encircles them with a luminous halo" (9). This passage occurs a few lines after the last one quoted above (9), as the narration continues to concern itself with the possibilities and limitations of several fields of vision. The first sentence unites the steeple and the umbels through this very consideration in natural proximity. The second and third sentences depart from this particular linking principle (depth of field) and replace it by one where the idea of comparable size and perspective has been muted, in favor of a more radical reliance on the properties of the writing as such. In effect, the link between the flowers and the belfry remains in terms of the contrast between the tallest and the smallest elements in the "frame." This link, however, must be abstracted, and has become much less obvious than the one introduced with it, where "the sun glistens" corresponds to "luminous halo."

We have thus moved from the contiguity created between two separate objects of description by a general narrative concept, a variation on the idea of point of view or focus, to one more intrinsic to the prose, belonging to its most basic component, the words. The rhyming takes place here between the similarity of images. At the same time a bond has been created between two aspects of verticality, steeple and flower, introducing the possibility of abstracting from different objects a common denominator. Another level of reading also shows that "covered with a fine white down," "encircled," and "luminous halo," parallel to "gray rectangle, stretched upwards, surmounted by a purplish triangle," are further anticipations of later, more explicit erotic imagery: penis and purplish glans, downy female genitals.

The other two elements of the initial "triangulation" (cascade, barn, see quote, p. 9 above) are linked to the church and to one another in rhyming schemes of a slightly different nature, though quite as effective. As the panoramic view of the valley continues, the barn becomes the next object of attention, called forth by means of the umbels, their downy stalks "flaring out like the ribs of an umbrella (*parapluie*) and supporting the platform of flowers" (9). The building is constructed with "vertical boards" (10), and its foundation "is barely flush with the ground"—in French *affleurer* ("to be flush with") contains *fleur* ("flower"). The word *umbel* is restated as *parapluie*; in French, *parapluie = ombrelle = umbel* (*ombelle*). The bond is created again in an undertone from the comparison of two vertical designs (stalk = vertical boards), but more specifically

also in terms of phonetic similarity together with related references (*lé plateau des* fleurs: affleure *tout juste le sol*). The text
now lingers on a description of the barn, whose main features
for the moment are some posters plastered on its side. In the
biggest and most recent among them "a few tears gape," of
which the widest "seems to have been enlarged purposely
[*à dessein*]" (11). The next sentence introduces the third element
in the initial trio: "At the foot of the falls a trough [*un bassin*]
has been dug out..." (11). Again we have a relationship
between the actions referred to (enlarged, dug out) and one
more obvious that results from homophony: *dessein, bassin*. The
transition back to the barn is executed in a comparable fashion.
The water's blueness "thickens gradually almost black at the
center of the trough" (11). This darkness elicits that pervading
the barn, where it takes some time for the eye "stuck to the
crack" (11) to become accustomed to "the semi-darkness" (11).
The relationship is now established through the imagery of
darkness, and it is this imagery, together with the continuing
erotic undertone, that allows the text to depart from this initial
referential triangle through a bird's-eye view, as it were. From
the penumbra in the barn we move to "the woods that cover
the slopes [*les flancs* = flanks] of the valley" (11) in which the
woods on the "flanks" of the valley represent a clear continuation
of the imagery of darkness.

The erotic undertones that were discernible through the
transitions previously seen linking the steeple with the flowers
and the flowers with the barn continue to obtain; indeed, they
become more specific, in this last group of relational images.
These connotations become clear only upon a rereading of the
novel after we have seen the entire composition, the complete
mosaic.

(a)   "a few tears" "The widest seems to have been enlarged
       purposely";
(b)   "At the foot of the falls a trough has been dug out";
(b')   "thickens gradually, almost black at the center of the trough";
(a')   "stuck to the enlarged crack," "semi-darkness";
(c)   "the woods that cover the slopes (flanks) of the valley";

The idea of enlarging the tear on the poster is echoed by that of water eroding, or digging a hole in the riverbed. The word *bassin,* which in French means both basin (trough) and pelvis, anticipates the back and forth movements of fornication, while being an image of the vulva; (b') suggests a thickening penis in the vulva and restates (a) and (b), and (a') repeats this imagery as the glance that penetrates the tear in the poster; (c) then is easily seen as an image of pubic hair, the valley as the woman's crotch and genitals. In confirmation of this reading we point out that the tear in the poster affords our first glimpse of sexual coupling, and that the relationship of water and love-making (as well as death and violence, an inseparable dyad in Simon) is constant throughout the novel.

The erotic substructure of the text has progressed in this "triangulation," from the idea of verticality (erect penis) to that of sexual congress (penetration). From the broader point of view of the investigation of representational modes, we see the camera eye defining the first triangulation and achieving an incomplete vision. This task is then perfected by the relational properties of the text, linking the same points. The completed movement draws a triangle, the schematic design for the female genitalia, while the "drawing" itself, the retreat to a panoramic view followed by a "penetration" towards the details of the picture, is a clear instance of representation as a metaphor for action, an image of the movement of coitus. In this scheme, (c'), as the view of the valley, represents a withdrawal. The sentence following (c') pursues the panoramic view in a description of the woods, echoing that of the beach in the postcard where their contour appears as "curves, gulfs, capes" (11); the parallelism of both situations is thus established from the beginning and suggests the closing of an introductory descriptive cycle. The general movement of the text is likewise established as of now in terms of an ever widening triangulation whose sweep will include a growing number of intermediate stages along the way, all originating from this first development. The postcard properly belongs to the resort sequence; it becomes the starting point of the depiction that contains the hamlet, itself providing, through the posters on the barn, the origin of the events in the industrial town. Similarly, this vision of the hamlet contains the source of all the secondary reinforcing episodes; the circus act (through the posters), the young boys and their activities, the rabbit, and so forth.

III *The Scenes*

As the momentum of the text grows, so will its capacity to invent; the principal cycles of action will be increasingly elaborated. In doing so, the medium of their appearance will be likewise examined in an effort to explore all possible relationships, to discover whether different techniques of representation reveal new links between the apparently disparate sequences. The language, however, will remain at all times the basic relational substructure, and the specificity of the action described will depend on the impetus that the text has so far acquired by means of self-reinforcing connotations.

The transitions examined above followed a twofold development, one involving what we have called the rhyming possibilities of the text, the other pertaining to a sustained erotic undercurrent. As opposed to such transitions, which occurred within the panoramic view of the hamlet, shifts from one important sequence to another will take place when the third structural element adds its weight to the operation of the other two: the nonverbal designs contained within the narrative, i.e., posters or snippets of film. That is why the first description of coitus in the barn takes place after these three elements come into play. There is a continued erotic undertone in the description of the barn's surroundings: the grass is rigid as "sabers or yataghans" (13), or "broken in two, the end hanging" (14); the lucern's leaves are oval and it has purple flowers.[4] The grass as sabers calls forth the widening of a hole in the barn's wall, by means of a knife and of the posters. A corner of the circus poster allows part of an older one to show where the silhouettes of an embracing couple appear; a chimney rises in a sky "black with clouds and smoke" (14). Here takes place the shift to the coitus inside the barn seen as "the flash of white skin contrasting against the blackness" (14). The progression is quite clear, each image containing a more explicit rendering of the coupling, with the poster containing both the suggestion (chimney against smoky sky) and the fact (silhouettes); the vision in the barn is now not only natural but inevitable. Furthermore, this passage has also introduced the first stage, as a fixed image, of the city episode (coitus in the alley).

Once initiated, these two sequences will soon reach their full development. The back and forth movement of the text as a pulsation of nature, parallel to the very rhythms of coitus, will sweep the surroundings of the barn, coming to rest each time at greater length on the scene therein. It will likewise elicit longer and more explicit portions of the lovemaking episode in the city. The pulsation communicates itself to every activity described in the narrative, to become an all-inclusive rendition of natural cycles, from procreation to death. The increasing sophistication of the settings wherein the main sequences take place, and that of their actors, produces a distortion of this basic development to the extent that the scene in the resort no longer includes the moment of coitus but only its aftermath. At this point, the rhythm belongs exclusively to the structure of representation rather than to its detail.

The correspondences and parallelisms are maintained throughout, in the manner just seen, by the self-generating momentum of the prose, whose patterns create the necessary connections between the three apexes of the triangle. These three points of departure have as of now been introduced (to p. 14) and will proceed in Part I to their first stage of completion, which marks for the barn and alley sequences the end of the coupling. The conclusions are seen as corresponding events: ejaculation outside of the woman's genitals in the barn; vomiting by the man in the alley. Examining the end of this first stage, we perceive that it contains an anticipation of the outcome of each entire sequence; in effect, the external ejaculation in the barn, seen as a loss of sperm, is also a loss of potential life; the consequences of this episode will be the drowning of the woman's child, an event which may in fact be taking place at that very moment; the constant returns to the river and the cascade maintain this eventuality as a background to the lovemaking. It is rendered explicit by the juxtaposition of the moment of ejaculation with a scene from a poster, showing a young domestic crying in her apron against a background of small dancing lamps in the night (search for the drowned girl). Likewise, the man's drunk-

enness, his vomiting and uncertain movements are a preview
of his later state, as he staggers to his hotel, bloody and disfigured. His bride sees him naked on their bed, his member
flaccid, as she stands in front of a mirror naked herself, her
desire frustrated. This inauspicious beginning of a marriage,
emphasizing the denial of lovemaking, also implies the denial
of conception and of a possible life.

The first image of the resort sequence, besides the postcard,
is that of a man standing by a door, listening and hesitating
to enter. Details of his appearance render it akin to that of an
erect penis. His body appears as a "black lump" (22) contrasting
with the red of the carpet. It is surmounted by "a purplish head"
with soft skin hanging "in folds" (22). The forearm extends
to the doorknob "at the level of the belly, like . . . a crutch" (23).
Behind the door, as we later find out, Corinne is lying naked
on a bed. The suggestion of sexual involvement between the
man and Corinne is clear. This involvement is not specified,
but we can surmise that it probably took place in the past. It is
this same man who will undertake the negotiations on behalf
of Corinne's son. At the end of Part I a poster shows the head
of a bejeweled woman, still beautiful, with two men facing
each other in the background, one of whom is the heavyset man
of the first image, and the other one, Lambert. The head of a
young man with fair, lamblike curls is between the woman and
the two men. The sexual undertone of the first man's description
and his later activities strongly imply that he is the father of
Corinne's illegitimate son. The solution to this story hinges on
the man's willingness to open the door, "penetrate" into Corinne's
presence, that is to say, resume his role as a father to save his
son. The coitus is not shown in this sequence because it is not
the origin of the problem (son's implication) but its consequence,
since Corinne offers herself to Lambert in the hope that he can
intervene on behalf of the young man. The center of the story
remains somewhat enigmatic, and it is the understanding of
this sequence that proves the most arduous because its development undergoes the greatest fragmentation. Its enigma is a
reflection of that which remains at the center of the entire
narrative, and its discontinuity also reflects closely the latter's
surface discontinuity.

Part I thus presents in the first steps of the mosaic's creation all the necessary elements toward an understanding of the fiction. The panoramic view of the hamlet contains all the starting points for the principal cycles of action; these cycles are initiated at the conjunction of the three basic elements of organization: connotative substructure (frequently erotic), verbal linkage (rhyming), and posters. In its progress the text will create alternate contiguities between each one of the main cycles, as well as between other individual episodes from the hamlet, establishing within all these elements an indissoluble metaphorical dependency whereby each cycle is as a reflection or an anticipation of the other. This development first becomes evident through the relationship between the postcard's overview of the beach with that of the valley. To restate this relationship, our first encounter with a character from the resort sequence takes place, as we saw, after a quick backward movement in which the woods of the valley are seen as the contours of a beach; the verbal linkage that produces the transition and the intensifying suggestive undertones of the text create the necessary conditions for the sequential shift. The cycles of the barn and the alley appear side by side from the beginning, elicited also by verbal bonds, as well as the strong, erotic content of the imagery and the introduction of the posters on the barn's walls. All these sequences reinforce one another to occupy longer portions of the text as we near the end of Part I. Here takes place, to complete the triangulation, the last panoramic view in this section showing the area surrounding the activities in the alley. Although the setting is drastically different, the description establishes clear correspondences between its elements and those of the first overview of the valley: The cascade is now a mine shaft whose tower recalls the church steeple. The continuous clanging of trains from a nearby railway siding further suggests the reverberating echo of bells in the valley. The mooing of cows and oxen from cattlecars brings to mind the cows herded through the hamlet, and a small locomotive "brokenwinded and archaic" (71) is the counterpart to the old woman pushing the broken-down baby carriage across the fields (secondary scene) (1). A canal cutting through the city is the cycle's answer to the river in the valley.

Concurrent with the development of these three cycles in Part I, the text pursues its admitted search for an organizing principle, which first appeared as the search for a visual vantage point quoted earlier from the three principal locations of the valley (steeple, cascade, barn). These indications of possible patterns become particularly striking when coincidences of color are underlined as if we were in fact engaged, together with the heavyset man at the conclusion, in the reconstruction of a puzzle. The first of these (on p. 20) links the oil stains on the motorcycle belonging to the man in the barn with the moss-covered stones at the bottom of the river. The surface coincidence of color points to a less obvious element in the structure of this particular episode: the little girl's drowning as a consequence of her mother's tryst. The next indication of this type (on p. 23) also underlines a color similarity, this time between the sawdust in the circus and the stockings of the woman in the alley. Here also this "invented" likeness stresses a less obvious relationship— that between the clown and the drunken groom.

Besides these imposed connections other ones less apparent pursue the introductory triangulation with respect to design rather than color. The most important is the subject of one entire secondary episode, that of the young boy trying to do a demonstration in geometry, and contains revealing information on the composition of the novel. The problem deals with a circle within a triangle, and is given in incomplete form. The episode is introduced by the poster of the clown doing his act in the circus ring under two converging spotlights, an image containing a triangle within a circle. The idea of triangulation finds its most explicit statement in this episode both because of the nature of the problem posed, and because it serves as a moment of transition to each one of the three main cycles. The drawing of the exercise, circle within triangle, is an accurate rendering of the condition of each cycle: the focus of the narrative is as a spotlight and creates a circle within the triangular pattern of the stories. In the barn sequence it consists of the man, the woman, and the child. In the alley sequence it is the groom, the woman, and the other man, later replaced by the bride. In the resort sequence there are several triangles: Brown, Corinne, and her son; Lambert, Corinne, and her son; and the two men at the café reaching an understanding again about Corinne's son.

The old woman appears in four of the six instances of the geometry sequence. Her presence is linked through it to each one of the main cycles, maintaining in all of them an aura of menace, not in any symbolic manner, but through the sheer force of her negative proximity, impervious, misshapen, black. She also undertakes the only visible violent action: the killing of the rabbit. It is in the second of these scenes involving the boy and his homework that a segment of film is introduced, showing Brown and another man engaged in some discussion in a bar. As the boy looks at it against the light, the old woman's silhouette appears between the two men: the implication could not be clearer. In the two instances of this episode when the old hag does not appear, the boy is visited first by a little girl, later by a young woman. Through it, therefore, circulate aspects of all the feminine presences in the fiction, from childhood to old age. The scene also contains the two principal forms of nonverbal representation, posters (it is introduced by one) and film.

As the novel progresses, the focus of attention is increasingly directed to the development of each sequence, while the frequency of their alternation diminishes significantly. The growing picture presents an ever wider range of possibilities for linkage and requires longer treatment of its main parts. In Part III, episodes continue uninterrupted over several pages. At the same time, the media of representation begin to acquire greater importance also, as if the text were imposing its own relational patterns on events whose mutual correspondences could go no further. The bonds created in Part I between the various segments of narrative have become a functioning vocabulary that comes into full play in the ensuing sections, serving to introduce later moments of the same sequences. It will no longer be necessary to have always the conjunction of connotation, image, and verbal link. These two latter elements have largely supplanted the first one as visible media of transition, not because it has disappeared, but rather because the entire text is now suffused with erotic implications or the menace of disaster, and the effect of this condition is manifest throughout.

Although seemingly at variance in its content with the three
central cycles, that of the circus, because of this very contrast,
provides a clear illustration of the metaphorical interdependency
of all the elements of the narrative. This sequence is introduced
early, together with the three central ones. The first image is
fixed (poster), and succeeds a description of shadows on the
face of the heavyset man in the resort hotel. It is itself followed
by the beginning of the coupling in the alley. Its appearance
in the entire first part will henceforth be linked to those two
sequences and their development. Its growth in importance
will likewise parallel that of the other scenes.

In the second part the circus act is situated at the center of
the novel's enigma. It is elicited by the picture of a lion on a
flashlight battery taken apart by two young boys, in an episode
whose structure reveals a primary aspect of that of the entire
narrative. The two boys, testing the energy of the battery, conclude: "It is dead" (76) and proceed to cut it apart. The image
of the lion allows a return to the clown poster on the barn,
and the latter calls forth another portion of the comic's performance. In this segment, the clown, focused upon by two
floodlights, is followed by two shadows in a double parody of
his gesticulations. The segment also contains the early moments
of his antics with one of his shoes, whose yawning upper part
turns it into a barking dog; this act becomes the basis for the
development of the entire sequence throughout the novel. The
number ends with laughter that "topples down" (*déferle*), suggesting the cascade, and through it introducing once more the
two boys. After repeating "it (she) is dead" (79), the older
one proceeds with the dismantling of the battery and breaks
a fingernail. He then uses a knife to cut through three tar-coated
concentric cylinders, finding a short section of film wrapped
around the last one. The film shows Corinne lying on the bed.

The repetition of "(She) is dead," with the cascade as a background, anticipates the little girl's accident. As we saw, the
boys will leave her in order to watch the two lovers in the barn.
The tar-coating of the battery's components corresponds to the
tar-covered boards of this same building. The parallelism may
be stated thus:

	(1) Lion's head		(1) Clown's poster
Battery	(2) 3 tar-coated cylinders	Barn	(2) Tar-coated boards
	(3) Film of Corinne		(3) Couple within

In this manner the enigma which the film seems to pose is transferred and solved. What the boys find at the center is a filmic
representation that refers to a corresponding event in the written
representation (narrative). The episode points to the activity
of the text as creator and solver of the mystery, to the structure of the novel as the enigma at its core. The suggestion of
pain (broken fingernail), and death, previews the unseen portion
of the three cycles in which violent incidents occur. The clown's
act is itself situated between two moments of this episode and
further underlines the idea of representation as the enigmatic
core of narration. The two parodic shadows that follow him
continue this ever receding play of mirrors, while implying also
that his performance is but the grotesque mimic of the action
of the novel.

The next appearance of the clown needs only the occasion
of a previously established link: it takes place after a passage
about the young boy and the geometry problem. The functioning surface element is the circle within the triangle; the un-
stated connection with the foregoing segment arises from the
fact that we have here also a young boy, and that he, too, has a
fragment of film (dealing with the resort sequence as well).
The echoes of the first series of transitions introducing the clown
will be transformed as the text proceeds, but they will always be
recognizable. The clown's act will be linked through the occasion of its appearance, as well as through its detail, with each
one of the main cycles. Thus, when the woman in the alley
sequence tries to prevent the groom from driving his car, given
his drunkenness, she expostulates: "Are you nuts Are you
completely nuts plastered (*beurré*) as you are" (106). These
words are echoed by the clown in the scene that follows: "Are
you not a bit nuts?" (*"Vous êtes pas un peu marteau non?"*)
(108), while his appearance (*beurre* = makeup[5] [plaster]) and
his actions (staggering) recall those of the groom. Similarly,
when the boys abandon the child with two little girls (multiple
triangulation), the circus act presents a grotesque reflection of

the incident. A clown dressed as Pierrot explains some problem: "The other clown shakes his head more and more emphatically agreeing ... and shouts ... oh, it's e-e-easy! The little girls nod in agreement ..." (184).

IV *The Sequences*

1. *From Fixed Images.* This growing reciprocity underlying each level of action, and all superficially diverse cycles, designates the activity of representing as the foundation of the novel's structure; it finds its most revealing manifestation in the role played therein by fixed or moving pictures. The concept of the camera eye is prevalent throughout the text, whether it is acknowledged or not. Backward travelings, panoramic views, zooms, choices of angles, all are widely used. All of the main sequences are grounded at some point in a fixed image, including that of the barn, which seems at first to be the most dependent on traditional direct narration.

The usefulness of static images is evidenced from the beginning, when the contiguity of a circus poster, a movie poster, and a live scene inside the barn allow an initial set of permutations to take place, their succession alternated in order to abstract common elements in their composition. Sequences will generally be seized by a fixed representation so that they may be explored in greater detail, and to allow the text to discover whether such designs are especially revealing. At the same time, a return to a fixed image means the reexamination of an unchanging point of reference; in a composition where there is no completed matrix to follow, the elements already established are invaluable guides. Such images will thus frequently be a reflection of the stage of development reached by the text at the moment when they appear. To underline the importance of several of these tableaux, their description is repeated almost verbatim in each one of the three parts of the novel. These images consist of two cinema posters in Parts I and II and a book cover in Part III, all related to the principal cycles of the narrative, according to the scheme on page 185 of this text.

In parts I and II the setting of the cinema is part of the one sequence among the three central ones not represented in the

	Part I	*Part II*	*Part III*
Setting of Image:	Cinema—industrial city	Cinema (barn) hamlet	Film studio
Poster I (This Week):	Corinne—anguished, crying / Two men facing each other; young man	Corinne—crying, anguished / Two men facing each other; young man	Filming of Corinne sequence
Poster II (Next Week):	Search in night / Anguished woman, woman crying / Man & Woman embrace in background	Two men fight / Man & Woman in alley embrace / Bride in despair / Bored groom	Book cover / Two men fight / Man & Woman in alley embrace / Bride in despair / Bored groom
Continuing Narrative	Same woman in both pictures of second poster	Same actor in both posters	Commentary by two boys of the coitus in the barn

posters. The continuing narrative makes two parallel statements. The second posters, although their action is different in detail, deal with the violent aftermath of the cycles to which they belong. The pattern of Part III continues that of the other two while it introduces the idea of ever receding mirror images, where one sequence is the film of the other one, which contains the first one as a novel, and so on. The ending of the pattern of Part III corresponds to the ending of the pattern of Part I, in that the two young boys are commenting on, within the novel's direct narrative, and as a part of the action of this narrative, events supposedly in a movie. The net effect of this scheme is that the various forms of representation cancel one another out, allowing only the total verbal medium of *Triptyque* to remain as the final structure. It is also for this reason that the variations in wording take place; minimal as they are, they permit the repetition to remain, while subjecting it to the momentum of the general narrative substructure. This substructure, for instance, creates the relationship between the poster of Corinne where she is seen first with "an anguished expression," and "a tearful gesture" (64), and the image of the woman in the second poster who appears first "her face anguished" (65) and then "her face tearful" (66). The sequence of adjectives is reversed in the second rendering of the Corinne poster, to correspond with that of the bride in the second poster: "Her eyes drowned in tears, her brows knitted, the design of her half-opened mouth, express anguish" (95). A close reading of the other variations in description suggests a similar tendency for these apparently static repetitions to reflect the pressures of the text.

2. *From Film.* The information on homology of structure of the main sequences afforded by contiguous posters is reiterated with even greater specificity through the novel's involved manipulation of films. Movies are shown in close proximity to other ongoing action, segments of film are viewed by characters belonging to the main narrative cycles, and some scenes are described in the process of being filmed. Likewise, consistent with the pattern of free circulation through the narrative of several forms of representation, moving pictures may become fixed images or paintings, or simply be continued as part of the general narration. Although both the barn and the industrial center sequences are on occasion seen as filmed events, it is that of the resort that is most consistently treated as a movie. It is also this story whose details we know least about, and whose plot requires the greatest amount of speculation on the

part of the reader. Indeed, this kind of reconstruction is what we must undertake with regard to the configuration of the entire novel.

The parallelisms established by the narrative through its own metaphorical development, and echoed by the interplay of static pictures, will be restated by filmic sequences, pursuing thus the pattern of triangulation from the point of view of representational media. The first segment of film to be introduced as such shows Corinne on the bed, and is examined by the young boy working on the geometry problem: as we pointed out above, it emphasizes the question of perspective as well as the concept of interpenetrating episodes. At the same time, this scene is the mirror image of the last one of the fiction, where a character in the movie sequence, to which he belongs, completes and then breaks up a puzzle whose subject is the hamlet. From the start then, film gives indications that go beyond the idea of proximate structures; the relationship between this medium and the encompassing narrative will likewise serve to underline basic aspects of the novel's organization, and in particular, those that concern the continuity and chronology of the narrative cycles.

One specific scene plays a crucial role in the chronological development of the novel's major stories. It takes place midway through the book (126–132) and follows a segment of the industrial center sequence: "The camera was probably hoisted to the top either of a steeple, or yet of one of those scaffoldings ... over a mine shaft ..." (126). In this position the camera gives a panoramic view of the town as "a vast dark beach" (126). In these lines we see an echo of the very first sight of the hamlet, where the belfry was one of the sighting points. The image of the city as a beach further suggests an overview of the Southern resort, and prepares for its appearance a few lines later. We witness a general triangulation whose apexes are the three centers of action of the novel, in preparation for a scene that will have a significant effect on its temporal development.

The description of the city quickly focuses on the figure of a motorcyclist in pursuit of the inebriated groom. The former lifts the machine onto the sidewalk, where he leaves it while he narrows on foot the distance to the other man. Here the incident is interrupted: "Having reached this point in the narrative, which

in fact closes a chapter, the woman interrupts her reading" (126).
It is also night outside of the reader's (Corinne's) room. The
scene proceeds now as direct narrative. But as the heavyset man
next door is described, his image is gradually transformed into
a painting, and then is animated once more. When Corinne now
pushes the mirrored door of a closet in order to see him, the
studio where the scene is being filmed is reflected on it. The
action continues for a few lines until the director cries "Cut"
(130). Various activities take place around the actors; the woman
picks up the novel once more and "leafs through backwards
(probably looking for a passage not well read or a detail to
which she had not paid sufficient attention)" (131). Now "The
bell announcing the imminent beginning of the performance has
been quiet for a few moments when there reaches in from outside
the din of two cars that seem to pursue one another, honking
noisily . . ." (131–132). We have been taken back to the city
sequence, at a moment previous to those encountered up to now.
The representational modifications concentrated in this passage
are: (1) the novel, read by the woman, containing the action
of the preceding sequence; (2) her companion's momentary
transformation into an oil portrait; (3) both of them as part of a
movie scene being taken; (4) the entire passage as part of a
film which is about to begin. Finally, (5) the text of the novel
contains, of course, all the rest. The central reflections of the
multiple *construction en abyme* (at whose center a mirror serves
to uncover the final artifice) seem again to cancel one another.
At this juncture important developments are initiated on two
levels: an anecdotal one with regard to Corinne's story, and the
temporal one with regard to the other two cycles. Brown now
says that he has managed to reach the police commissioner on
whom the fate of the woman's son depends. Here also the other
two stories are turned back to the moments preceding their first
appearance in the novel. This focus of temporal and anecdotal
activity is rendered by its metaphorical counterpart: increased
representational transformations.

It is nevertheless the filmic sequence that seems to hold the
key to the continuity of the hamlet and city cycles. The car honks
that follow this passage are sounded by wedding guests, arriving with the groom at the bar where he is to meet the woman

with whom he will make love in the alley. Shortly after, we see the farm domestic entrusting her daughter to the two boys, before she goes to meet her lover in the barn. As for the movie sequence itself, a few pages later we are given what may be taken as its opening scenes, played in a barn opposite the church in the hamlet (another triangulation): *"LE COMMISSAIRE BASTIANINI"* ("Superintendent Bastianini")[6] (238); some fragments of this film suggest the usual detective hero yarn.

Other uses of film further direct our attention to what is the true plot of the novel. The manipulation of segments of film by the young boys in the hamlet sequence is an anticipation of Brown's work on the picture puzzle at the end. We have already seen how in another instance one of these fragments led directly to the core of the novel's enigma.[7] Here the boys try to find the proper sequence in which to organize their strips of negative, attempting to understand the plot from these disparate pieces. Engaged in this task, one of them picks up an apple from the ground and, after careful examination, bites it, only to spit out the piece in disgust, having presumably found a worm in it or some internal rot.[8] This detail recalls the early scene where the student working on the geometry problem draws inside the triangle a slightly flattened circle "like the contour of an apple" (24). The two boys' activity is thus compared to the problem of the triangle and linked with the general organization of the narrative, while a return to the beginning is initiated. This return is further signaled by two other strips of film: the first one is new and shows a rebellious-looking young man, presumably Corinne's son, flinging about in front of her his textbooks and notebooks, with Brown sitting in the background; the second one, previously seen, shows Brown standing by the closed door. The first scene confirms our early assumption that Brown is probably the young man's father, while it is also related (through the textbooks in disarray) to the episode of the boy working out the geometry problem. The scene of the man at the door also refers us to that earlier moment, since it is that strip of film that the student takes out of his pocket and examines in the light. A further relationship between these two fragments is revealed at the end of the novel when Brown, in an exasperated gesture, disperses his just completed puzzle with a movement that corresponds to that of the young man throwing down his books.

Only at the end of the novel are its multiple triangular relationships entirely revealed. We then conceive its action to be intimately linked to the activity that a triangulation implies, which is that of defining a height or a direction. The novel's plot is, on one level, the composition of its representational mosaic. In another, it is the very *activity* of creating this structure. In previous novels the composition was the real plot. Here the effort to discover this composition creates it and is the ultimate coordinating force of the fiction.

Conclusion

OUR insistence throughout this study on the activity of language per se as the foundation of the narrative and on composition as the true plot was meant in some sense to prepare for the last three, less accessible works. Simon's writing, as I hope to have shown, has constantly moved toward increasingly self-conscious creation. His style has changed radically. No longer do we have in his later novels long, intricate sentences, replete with parentheses, dominated by present participles. Instead, especially as of the third part of *The Battle of Pharsalus,* we read rather short statements, minimally qualified, impersonal. Such apparent straightforwardness, however, is, as we saw, a deceptive surface stretched tight over exceptional intensity, powerful concision. The structure of these last novels depends much more on the echoes, the connotations, the requirements of *words,* than it does on whatever events these words may be describing.

The cross-referential patterns of the language of these works, the foundation of their composition, have reached a high degree of intricacy and require of the reader exceptional attentiveness. In my examination I have tried to delineate what I take to be the underlying movement of each text, by simply *describing* what the words *do.* One may consider the reading of the first five novels as a necessary preparation to the reading of the last three; it has been the direction of this study.

Parallel to the growing autonomy assumed by language, the role of elements at first decisive to the composition, such as love and death, has gradually diminished. Already in *The Wind* language and memory mitigated and transformed their impact. I have felt this evolution to be the most important factor in Simon's writing. Consequently, other facets, such as possible mythical or even esoteric substructures have been merely hinted at. On them also much work remains to be done.

191

Notes and References

Preface

1. Note on *Entretiens*: This issue of *Entretiens* reached me after the body of my text was completed; I was indeed pleased to find in it confirmation, from M. Simon's own statements to Ludovic Janvier, of some ideas which I put forth in this study.

2. (Claude Simon, "Réponses a Ludovic Janvier" in *Entretiens*, No. 31.) From Ricardou, Jean, *Le Nouveau Roman*, p. 181. My translation.

Chapter One

1. Claude Simon, *The Wind* (New York: George Braziller, Inc., 1959), pp. 10–11. All future references are to this edition.

2. This term was used by Bruce Morrissette in *Les Romans de Robbe-Grillet* (Paris: Editions de Minuit, 1963).

3. Italics mine.

4. A French notary executes deeds, deals with sales of real estate, with marriage contracts, etc.

5. The subtitle, "Tentative de restitution d'un retable baroque," does not appear in the English version. This translation is my own.

6. See first quotation: "tossed about like floating corks without direction or perspective" (pp. 10–11).

7. See below for the significance of green.

8. Contrary to Sturrock's statement: "since in *Le Vent* it would still seem that what we have to deal with are the narrator's perceptions and not his memories." *The French New Novel*, p. 60.

9. Regression of rooms—regression toward the past, toward his own childhood. An idea reminiscent of the play within a play in *Hamlet* and a favorite device of Baroque drama (e.g., Rotrou's *Saint Genet*). It will appear frequently in Simon's subsequent novels. Gide called it *"construction en abyme"* and saw its origin in heraldry, an interpretation later disputed by Morrissette.

10. Rose = Virgin Mary; Montes = Jesus.

11. *Pommele* ("dappled"): green (*Pomme*–["Apple"]).

12. The *V* is particularly apt as a pictograph of violence (arrow, ax, etc.) or sex (see *The Battle of Pharsalus*).

Chapter Two

1. Claude Simon, *The Grass*, trans. Richard Howard (New York: George Braziller, 1960), p. 14. All future references are to this edition.

2. Sturrock, p. 63, p. 77, etc.

3. The contrast is not rendered in the English version: "the train stopped" would have done so. (*"le train arrêté maintenant," L'Herbe*, p. 21.)

4. These statements are not included in the English text. They should appear on p. 99. The translation is my own: *"De quel droit? Elle . . . de quel droit!," L'Herbe*, p. 118.

5. "Streaming" is *"pleurant"* in the original, that is, "crying."

6. The French has *"se rappellera"* (124): "will remember." The change in verb tenses is radical.

7. The French has *"cette sorte de végétation"* (249) ("this kind of vegetation") which is not translated into English—the idea of a fusion with the surrounding plant life is more obvious in the original.

8. *"s'en fichant pas mal"* (22), (translated into "heedless"), conveys in French a much stronger feeling on the part of Louise, the observer, more adequately rendered as "not giving a damn."

9. The English version gives *"se trouvent là"* (91) as "were . . . there"; the change to the present is therefore lost.

10. "Shutters" suggest hinges, those articulating one portion of the text with another.

Chapter Three

1. Claude Simon, *Orion aveugle* (Geneva:: Editions Skira, 1970). This statement belongs to the introduction, ten unnumbered pages reproducing a text in the author's script. The translation is my own.

2. Claude Simon, *The Flanders Road*, trans. Richard Howard (New York: George Braziller, Inc., 1961), pp. 279–280. All future references are to this edition.

3. The French is here more explicit: *"son chose rose"* ("her pink thing"), *La Route des Flandres*, p. 257.

4. Tradition appears figuratively as a crust. The new uniforms issued to Georges and his companions are a *"carapace"* ("shell"). The dead horse is covered by a crust of mud. The vulva *"moule"* ("mussel") is an encased softness and brings forth both life and death.

5. This picture may be seen as another aspect of Georges's own coitus with Corinne. Details of its description reinforce the idea of "riding" and other gestures reminiscent of the print.

6. Simon has said that the novel is structured in the form of a cloverleaf with the decaying horse at its center. See Sturrock, p. 76. The horse is also a mythical image of death.

7. As Georges converses with his father prior to leaving for the front, the latter's glasses reflect repeated turns of the plow in a nearby field.

8. Simon will use this same technique later, notably in *The Palace*.

9. Not rendered in English: *"j'avais l'habitude je veux dire j'habitais l'attitude je veux dire j'habitudais de monter . . . ," La Route des Flandres*, p. 311. The translation can only be tentative: "I had the habit of, I mean I inhabited the attitude of, I mean I habituated to mount. . . ."

Chapter Four

1. At the beginning of the Civil War, probably late July or August, 1936.

2. Claude Simon, *The Palace*, translated by Richard Howard (New York: George Braziller, 1963), p. 13. All future references are to this edition.

3. Not translated: *"reflets émeraude," Le Palace*, p. 9.

4. Note the map's position, above the typewriter, mentioned in a parenthesis.

5. *"¡EL CRIMEN HA SIDO FIRMADO!," p.* 46.

6. Entry through map of the city and parenthesis.

7. There is a slight change in the beginning of Chapter 4, not rendered in the English version. End of Chapter 3: *"Le monde entier était gris, terne, pesant, humide . . . ," Le Palace*, p. 141. Beginning of Chapter 4: *"Le monde entier était sans couleurs, pesant, humide,"* p. 143.

8. Leaden gray lines—bullets.

9. We are here reminded of the mitigating effect of language in the death scene of *The Wind*.

10. Columbus—colombe—pigeon. Columbus is standing on a pillar. Pillar = column of names.

11. The *Columna de Hierro* was an anarchist group fighting at the front and also active behind the lines. Fierro is of course the old spelling of hierro (iron) and easily becomes Ferro to create the correspondence with "Fósforo Ferrero."

12. That is, in the original version. See note 7.

13. Analysis, sputum, blood, urine.

14. The center of the enigma, here in chapter IV, corresponds in

another way to the central part of chapter II (in the restaurant):
parentheses suddenly proliferate around the "key."

15. "Ready to tear" is my own translation of *"prêt à déchirer"*
(p. 167), not given in English.

16. "Do not tolerate shirkers."

17. The French text has *"macrocéphale"* ("macrocephalic"). Sturrock states (p. 62, p. 74) that the narrator-student commits suicide
at the end. We see no evidence of this; on the contrary, all indications point merely to a metaphorical death. There is no structural
necessity for a true suicide. Sturrock himself admits (p. 74) that
such an act is unique among Simon's protagonists.

Chapter Five

1. Claude Simon, *Histoire*, trans. Richard Howard (New York:
George Braziller, Inc., 1968), p. 1. All future references are to this
edition.

2. Cf. *The Palace*.

3. The novel begins with a lower-case letter: "l'une d'elles . . . ,"
Histoire, p. 9. The English version does not: "One of these. . . ."

4. We indicate chapter numbers merely for convenience in our
study.

5. There follow here several paragraphs dealing with the mass,
served at home for the narrator's dying mother.

6. "Distinguishing" in the English version; "perceiving" is my
own translation.

7. Some suggestiveness is lost in translation. "A vague furrow"
is *"un vague sillon bordé de lèvres molles,"* *Histoire*, p. 118.

8. In her youth, the narrator's mother lives for two years with her
husband on an almost uninterrupted ocean voyage. Her proximity to
water then maintains the relation, water = sex.

9. Rivière = River.

10. [The twin loops of the *l*] rendered in English as "the double
cursive." It is important, as our reading shows, that [*l*] remain.

Chapter Six

1. O is at times the younger narrator; at times, his uncle Charles;
both participate interchangeably in the same action. O is even occasionally the deceiving woman.

2. Cf. Jean Ricardou, "La Bataille de la phrase" in *Pour une
théorie du Nouveau Roman*. M. Ricardou gives a detailed analysis
of the correspondence between Valéry's stanza and the opening of

the novel. The chapter contains much enlightening material on *The Battle of Pharsalus.*

3. See in the epigraph "Your winged arrow finds its mark." Claude Simon, *The Battle of Pharsalus,* trans. Richard Howard (New York: George Braziller, Inc., 1971), p. 25. All future references are to this edition.

4. The event is rewritten. Time is subservient to the decision of words.

5. In French: "Le pinceau d'un autre projecteur se déplacait sautait brusquement d'un spectateur à l'autre . . . ," *La Bataille de Pharsale,* p. 24. "The *brush* of another spotlight, etc." The transition between the artist's studio and the Music Hall is thus clearer.

6. Cf. Jean Ricardou in *Pour une théorie du Nouveau Roman,* pp. 150–153.

7. See note 6.

8. The statements are in French more integrated to the tone of the passage: *"Eaux mortes"* (p. 18) for "Dead secret," *"la mort dans l'âme"* (p. 18) for "dead tired."

9. Supporting texts are given in italics the first time and then are run into the normal script.

10. Note the doube *V* of the name.

11. We use this term in the sense of "created" vocabulary of the narrative.

12. "Dogs' heads" in Greek.

13. Jean Ricardou, *Le Nouveau Roman,* p. 183.

14. Cf. Ricardou.

15. In French, tool = *outil.*

Chapter Seven

1. Published by Viking Press as *Conducting Bodies,* in July 1974, while this manuscript was in press. I am grateful to the publisher for having made a copy of the galleys of *Conducting Bodies* available to me. The translations, however, are my own.

2. A portion of this text was quoted in the Introduction to our reading of *The Flanders Road.*

3. Claude Simon, *Orion aveugle* (Geneva: Editions Albert Skira, 1970).

4. Claude Simon, *Les Corps conducteurs* (Paris: Editions de Minuit, 1971), p. 8. All future references are to this edition.

5. The lowered trousers "cross" both legs; also, the humiliation felt by the man is as a cross to bear.

6. Cf. *Le Nouveau Roman,* p. 184.

7. The heraldic animals of the coat of arms are a condor and a leopard: airplane-jungle.

8. *Orion aveugle* contains it.

Chapter Eight

1. We soon learn that the woman is Corinne and the man Lambert (see *Histoire*).

2. Claude Simon, *Triptyque* (Paris: Editions de Minuit, 1973), p. 7. All future references are to this edition.

3. Ricardou also uses this term (see *Le Nouveau Roman*), although in a more specific context.

4. The three basic colors of *Triptyque* are black, red, and white (three basic colors of the Mother Goddess; three basic colors of the alchemical work). Red and its various shades from pink to purple are associated with sex (and its counterpart, death, or violence).

5. *"Beurré"* in slang means drunk and in normal usage "buttered" —an apt description of the clown's makeup.

6. The fragments that we see of this movie, containing a payoff, etc., are as subversive of the common detective story as the organization of *Triptyque* is of the standard work of fiction.

7. Film inside flashlight battery.

8. This detail points to the invisible scenes at the center of the novel, those not described, where the violence and death take place.

Selected Bibliography

PRIMARY SOURCES

Works by Claude Simon

Le Tricheur. Paris: Editions de Minuit, 1945.
La Corde raide. Paris: Editions de Minuit, 1947.
Gulliver. Paris: Calmann-Lévy, 1952.
Le Sacre du Printemps. Paris: Calmann-Lévy, 1952.
Le Vent, tentative de restitution d'un retable baroque. Paris: Editions de Minuit, 1957.
L'Herbe. Paris: Editions de Minuit, 1958.
La Route des Flandres. Paris: Editions de Minuit, 1960.
Le Palace. Paris: Editions de Minuit, 1962.
Femmes (sur vingt-trois peintures de Joan Miró), tirage limité. Paris: Editions Maeght, 1966.
Histoire. Paris: Editions de Minuit, 1967.
La Bataille de Pharsale. Paris: Editions de Minuit, 1969.
Orion aveugle. Geneva: Editions Albert Skira, 1970.
Les Corps conducteurs. Paris: Editions de Minuit, 1971.
Triptyque. Paris: Editions de Minuit, 1973.

SECONDARY SOURCES

BERGER, YVES. "L'Enfer, le temps." *La Nouvelle Revue Française,* 97 (January, 1961). Principally on *The Flanders Road.*

BLOCHMICHEL, JEAN. *Le Présent de l'indicatif.* Paris: Gallimard, 1963. On several authors of the Nouveau Roman. For Simon, deals mostly with problems of time structure in *The Flanders Road.*

BOURDET, DENISE. *Brèves rencontres.* Paris: Bernard-Grasset, 1963. "Image de Paris: Claude Simon." *La Revue de Paris,* 1 (January, 1961).

BROMBERT, VICTOR. "Technicien de roman: Claude Simon." *Les Nouvelles Littéraires,* 1739 (December 29, 1960).

CAMPOS, ALONSO. "Una conversación con Claude Simon." *Cultura Universitaria,* 82–83 (Julio–dic., 1960). Simon gives some interesting information on how he writes.

DEGUY, MICHEL. "Claude Simon et la représentation." *Critique*, 187 (December, 1962). On the predominance of the visual.

DESCAVES, PIERRE. "Réalités du roman." *La Table Ronde*, 157 (January, 1961). On *The Flanders Road*.

ENTRETIENS, 31 (1972). Principally interesting for the biographical information; the article "Réponses de Claude Simon à quelques questions écrites de Ludovic Janvier" contains much information by Simon on his methodology.

ESPRIT. "Numéro special sur le Nouveau Roman." (July–August, 1958).

FITCH, BRIAN. "Participe présent et procédés narratifs chez Claude Simon" in Matthews, J. H., *Un Nouveau Roman: recherches et traditions, la critique étrangère*. Paris: M. J. Minard, 1964. Some interesting thoughts on Simon's use of the present participle.

FOURNIER, EDITH. "*Le Palace* de Claude Simon." *Médiations* (Summer, 1963). Sees "the student" and "the city" as the narrative foci of the novel.

JANVIER, LUDOVIC. *Une Parole exigeante, le Nouveau Roman*. Paris: Editions de Minuit, 1964. Emphasizes the "existential" implications of Simon's novels (to *The Palace*). "Le temps d'une histoire." *La Quinzaine Littéraire*, 25 (April 1–15, 1967).

JUIN, H. "Les secrets d'un romancier." *Les lettres Françaises* (October 6, 1960).

LESAGE, LAURENT. "Claude Simon et l'Ecclésiaste." *La Revue des Lettres Modernes*, 94–99.

LUCCIONI, G. "*Histoire* de Claude Simon." *Esprit* (Sept. 1967). Sees in the novel two superimposed narratives: the story of the narrator, and that of a mythical "young girl" (later mother, etc.).

MERCIER, VIVIAN. *The New Novel*. New York: Farrar, Straus and Giroux, 1971.

MORRISETTE, BRUCE. "The New Novel in France." *Chicago Review*, 3 (Winter–Spring, 1962).

NADEAU, M. *Le Roman français depuis la guerre*. Paris: Gallimard, coll. Idées, 1963.

OLLIER, CLAUDE. "*L'Herbe* de Claude Simon," *La Nouvelle Revue Française*, 73 (January, 1959). Ollier sees in this novel an effort to capture the irresistible march toward death.

PINGAUD, BERNARD. "Sur *la Route des Flandres*." *Les Temps Modernes*, 178 (February, 1961). For Pingaud, Georges remains transparent, a mirror reflecting the other characters. Most perceptive on Simon's transitions between narrative blocs.

RICARDOU, JEAN. *Problèmes du Nouveau Roman*. Paris: Editions du

Seuil, 1967. *Pour une théorie du Nouveau Roman.* Paris: Editions du Seuil, 1971. *Le Nouveau Roman.* Paris: Editions du Seuil, 1973. Ricardou has read Simon with the closest attention. His most illuminating study is that on *The Battle of Pharsalus.*

ROUSSET, JEAN. "Trois romans de la mémoire: Butor, Pinget, Simon," *Cahiers Internationaux de Symbolisme,* 1965.

SEYLAZ, JEAN-LUC. "Du *Vent* à *La Route des Flandres,* la conquête d'une forme romanesque." *La Revue des Lettres Modernes,* no. 94–99. Emphasis on time.

STURROCK, JOHN. *The French New Novel.* New York: Oxford U. Press, 1969. Like Ricardou's, an invaluable study, includes *Histoire.*

WEST, PAUL. *The Modern French Novel.* London: Hutchinson, 1963.

The work of Claude Simon has become the focus of an ever increasing number of articles. I indicated in the preface the studies I found to be the most perceptive. Of comparable interest among those above are the articles of B. Pingaud, M. Deguy, C. Ollier, and B. T. Fitch.

Index

(The works of Simon are listed under his name)

Achilles, 86, 122, 126, 134
Aphrodite, 62
Apuleius: *The Golden Ass,* 110, 115, 135
Atrides, 62

Bacchus, 62

Caesar, 115, 121, 135, 137, 138, 140; *The Civil Wars,* 115, 121
Caravaggio, Polidoro da, 142
Centaur, 62
Chazal, Malcolm de, 56, 66
Chiron, 62
Columbus, 85, 195n10

Dike, 22
Du Guesclin, 100

Entretiens, 193n1
Estang, Luc, 95

Heidegger, Martin, 140

Janvier, Ludovic, 95
Jesus, 24, 163
Juno, 22

Luther, Martin, 56

Marx, 78
Mauriac, Claude, 195
Morrissette, Bruce, 193n2, 193n8

Orion, 162, 163, 165, 166

Patroclus, 76, 86
Picasso, 166
Pierrot, 184
Poussin, 148, 162, 163, 165
Proust, 134

Rameses II, 41
Ricardou, Jean, 193n2, 196n2
Rilke, R. M., 107, 117

Simon, Claude
  WORKS:
  Battle of Pharsalus, The, 120-45, 147, 148,, 167, 172, 191
  Corps conducteurs, Les, 146-66, 167, 171, 172
  Flanders Road, The, 54-72, 73, 75, 76, 124, 146, 148
  Grass, The, 35-53, 54, 57, 73
  Histoire, 54, 95-119, 120, 122, 124, 148
  Orion aveugle, 146, 148
  Palace, The, 54, 73-94, 95, 97, 117, 118, 124, 147
  Triptyque, 135, *167-90*
  Wind, The, 15-34, 35, 36, 44, 54, 57, 97, 191
Stalin, 78
Sturrock, John, 193n8, 196n17

Valéry, Paul, 18, 122; *Graveyard by the Sea,* 122
Vercingétorix, 140
Vinci, Leonardo da, 56